...fe of Step... and mother of his five, six or possibly seven children. Her first book, *Mrs Fry's Diary* – a frank and revealing insight into a year in the Fry household – received great critical acclaim and provoked a good deal of bemusement. Her talents are many and varied – her Spam Bourguignon has to be tasted to be believed, her poetry is unlike anything you will ever read and her childcare techniques are legendary. And she manages all of this while carrying out her somewhat demanding wifely duties (especially on a Sunday morning).

When not being a domestic goddess, literary marvel and carrying Stephen home from the pub, Edna likes to spend her time on Twitter (largely to keep an eye on her husband's fanciful pronouncements), where she has won the prestigious Shorty Award for Funniest Tweeter. She also likes tea. A lot.

HOW TO HAVE AN
ALMOST
PERFECT MARRIAGE

How to Have

an

ALMOST

PERFECT

MARRIAGE

by

Mrs Stephen Fry

unbound

First published in hardback in 2012
This paperback edition published in 2014

Unbound
4—7 Manchester Street   Marylebone   London   W1U 2AE
www.unbound.co.uk

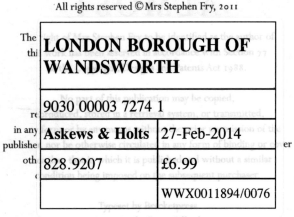

LONDON BOROUGH OF WANDSWORTH	
9030 00003 7274 1	
Askews & Holts	27-Feb-2014
828.9207	£6.99
	WWX0011894/0076

Typeset by Bookcraft

Lettering by Ryan Gillard
Art direction by Mecob

A CIP record for this book is available from the British Library

ISBN 978-1-78352-024-4 (trade PB)
ISBN 978-1-908717-09-2 (trade HB)
ISBN 978-1-908717-10-8 (ebook)

Printed in England by Clays Ltd, Bungay, Suffolk

For my dear husband and children, without whom things would have been so much simpler.

Contents

Contents

Forewarning

An almost perfect book, written in almost perfect English
by an almost perfect spouse.

— Stephen Fry

Introduction

Do you, Edna Constance Bathsheba, take Stephen
John Elvis to be your lawfully wedded husband?
I did.

EADER, I married him. Or e-reader, I married him, if
you prefer. For after many, many years of marriage and
many, many children, I've decided it's only fair to
share my unparalleled expertise and deepest secrets with you
in this invaluable guide.

Of course, the 'him' to whom I refer is my current husband,
Stephen. You may be aware of his numerous books, his countless television shows and his enormous intellect. You probably
know he spends his time travelling endlessly, attending operas,
meeting famous stars of stage and screen and visiting tribes-
people in the remotest corners of the globe. That's if you read
all that rubbish he writes on Twitter, anyway – honestly, that
man's imagination!

If you frequent the Dog & Duck, however, you'll know the
truth. Or the Red Lion. Or Kevin's kebab van. Because that's
where you'll almost certainly find him. Not dining at the Ritz

or filming something about wizards in New Zealand and certainly not at home helping me take care of our children!

Of course, someone like you can't realistically expect to have a marriage as perfect as ours, which is why I've called this book *How To Have an Almost Perfect Marriage*, but whether you're a husband-, wife- or divorcee-to-be or just simply Fry-curious, you'll learn everything you need to know, and quite a lot you don't, about the most wonderful years of your life as these nine chapters guide you through every aspect of marriage from proposal to divorce.

WHAT IS MARRIAGE?

According to Vaguelytruepedia.com, marriage as an institution has been around for centuries. The word itself harkens back to Medieval times, when any couple declaring eternal love for each other were ritually transported through the streets, exposed to ridicule and scorn in an open coach known popularly as the 'mad carriage'. Over the years, this became shortened to 'mad rage' and finally lengthened again to 'marriage'.

Marriage as we know it (i.e. with wedding dresses and confetti as opposed to straightjackets and rotting vegetables) was invented in 1963 by the writers of popular US situation comedy *Behitched* as a narrative device to create conflict. Up to that point, if a couple appeared in a television show they were almost certainly living in sin, gay or at the very least, mixed race (interestingly, the first inter-marriage kiss ever broadcast occurred in the long-running science-fiction series,

Star Trek, when William Shatner married Mr Spock's rather hairy half-sister in the episode *The Stubble with Sybil*).

WHY GET MARRIED?

Statistically, 100 per cent of divorces start with marriage. And yet there are still hundreds of thousands of weddings each year – why?

Well, people get married for all sorts of reasons – security, social convention, pregnancy, boredom, fear of being alone, even love. Personally, I fancied a new hat and Stephen was nearby. Of course, we all hope to have a string of marriages to increasingly attractive and wealthy partners, but the reality for many couples is that their marriage will endure for the rest of their lives – a chilling thought and one worth considering before entering into what is, after all, a legally-binding contract (*see section on how to get out of legally-binding contracts*). While this can seem daunting, it's equally important to remember that compared with being systematically abused in a nursing home or dying alone in a skip, spending your twilight years with your spouse can be relatively acceptable. Personally, I think it's always good to see an elderly couple walking down the street hand in hand – it stops them falling over.

There is also the question of money. The tabloids are full of warring celebrity couples for whom the rather unseemly battle for financial remuneration has muddied the marital waters and allowed them to lose sight of the reason they were getting divorced in the first place.

And it can be easy to get carried away with the romance of a wedding – the church, the dress, the horse-drawn carriage, the free bar. People even use the phrase 'fairy tale wedding' although very few use the phrase 'fairy tale marriage' – unless they're referring to the original, traditional fairy tale which was generally a pretty gruesome adventure without a happy ending.

This book is intended as a guide not only for those couples about to enter into a state of holy matrimony but also those couples already in a state. If you and your spouse are sitting there, cosily imagining that you have nothing to learn from the following pages, I recommend you attempt the following short quiz and I'm quite confident that you will feel differently by the time you've finished.

HOW PERFECT IS YOUR MARRIAGE?

HIS QUESTIONS

1. When was the last time you forgot your wife's birthday?
   a) I never forget her birthday – the date is etched eternally on my heart, together with our wedding anniversary, the day we first met and her shoe size.
   b) I only once forgot her birthday but I never will again. Luckily, the surgery was a success.
   c) I know when Elvis was born – does that count?

2. Your wife has bought a new dress but looks terrible in it. What do you say to her when she asks how she looks?
   a) Gorgeous, darling, as always.
   b) I'm not sure it shows off your amazing figure to its very best, my sweet.
   c) Hahahahahahahahahahahaahahahahaahahahaha

3. At a party, you notice a good-looking man eyeing up your wife. What do you do?
   a) Nothing. Just feel proud that he's noticed how attractive she is.
   b) Give him a dirty look and steer her towards the vol-au-vents.
   c) Ask if he's ever considered laser eye surgery.

4. Your wife wants you to go with her to the cinema this evening to see the latest Hollywood romantic comedy. What do you do?
   a) You go along with her to watch it. The most important thing to you is that she's happy, even if it is inane, shallow drivel.
   b) You agree to go but pop out in the afternoon and set fire to the cinema.
   c) You agree to go but pop out in the afternoon, set fire to the cinema and frame your wife for it.

HER QUESTIONS
1. How on earth do you manage to put up with him?

Right, now that's all sorted, let's proceed, shall we? Pop the kettle on, put your feet up, turn the page and let's begin your seemingly unlikely journey to an Almost Perfect Marriage ...

CHAPTER ONE

Finding Mr (or Miss) Right

Please note, this chapter is aimed at unmarried readers —
I'm afraid it's too late for the rest of you, dears.

BEFORE YOU get married, there is one very important thing you must do – locate your future spouse. Without him or her, the event is likely to be a bit of a damp squib. So, how should you go about this onerous task? I'm glad you asked …

WHERE TO LOOK

According to research, one of the best places to meet your future husband or wife is the supermarket (this is especially true if you're seeking a life partner with a career in the check-out or shelf-stacking sectors). Sadly, this is becoming less true as more and more people are choosing to have their weekly shop delivered for a small extra cost, leaving only the poor, the disorganised and the computer illiterate to patrol the aisles. Fortunately, that still leaves plenty of candidates to choose from, provided you're not too fussy.

So how should you go about this 'partner-shopping' as I like to call it? Simply wandering aimlessly around your local supermarket for hours on end will provoke suspicion among customers and store detectives so it's important that you have a clear strategy. First, you need to identify your almost ideal partner and choose your hunting ground accordingly. Is she a Waitrose kind of girl? Is he a Tesco or a Sainsbury's guy? Does everything about her scream Asda? Once you've selected the right establishment, take a deep breath, put some clothes on and pop along. Evenings are generally the best time unless you have a preference for the unemployed or elderly but do try to avoid Saturday evenings if possible – we don't want to appear too desperate, do we?

When you enter the store, do so confidently with a light, breezy air. You're saying 'I'm here merely to do my shopping, not to find the man or woman of my dreams, although should that opportunity present itself I wouldn't necessarily run away screaming.' To this end, it's important to appear open and friendly – a bright smile will help attract a possible partner although too big a smile could result in him or her running away screaming. On a scale of 1 to 10, with one being a slight curling of the lip and 10 being Jack Nicholson in *The Shining*, I would recommend about a three.

Take a basket (a trolley suggests that you have a family, particularly if you have a small child in the seat) and casually parade up and down the aisles. If you are looking for a wife you could try the chocolate department, if it's a husband you seek, the beer section, but there's one area more likely than any other to bear fruit (other than the fruit aisle) – the ready meals freezer. So many of the great romances of our age have been sparked by hands meeting accidentally over a roast chicken dinner for one. I wonder where Prince William and dear Princess Kate would be now without Findus Crispy Pancakes?

Having successfully engineered your 'chance' meeting, all that's left is for you to engage in fascinating conversation, discover numerous common interests, fall madly in love and book the church – easy!

INTERNET DATING

A modern alternative to the supermarket is the internet (also for shopping, should the urge take you). Whether you prefer social networking or dating sites, looking for a prospective partner on the world wide web can be a minefield. I have an acquaintance, let's call her Edwina, who spent months chatting on the website *SuperspouseMe.com* to someone who claimed to be a door-to-door double-glazing salesman called Neville only to finally discover he was, in actual fact, a door-to-door double-glazing salesman called Neville. Naturally, she assumed he'd been lying as so many do from the safety and anonymity of their computer keyboards. You can imagine her disappointment. Another acquaintance, let's call him Stefan, was surprised to find that the leggy 22 year old blonde part-time lap-dancer from Lytham St Annes was in fact the Archbishop of Canterbury.

Even if the person in whom you have any interest has given their real identity and occupation they may still not be being completely honest about their relationship status – they may already have a partner or even a spouse, but how can you tell? Examine their online photograph closely. The following should raise your suspicions – a white mark around their ring finger, a wedding ring around their ring finger, his and hers towels hanging in the background or a marriage certificate hanging in the background.

If you find dating sites a little 'full-on' and you prefer a more casual approach, there are several social networking sites that allow you to make contact with like-minded (i.e. socially inept) people such as yourself. The popular friendship site Facebook, for example, allows you to exchange pleasantries, banalities and farm animals in your pursuit of eternal love.

If your social and literary skills are even more basic, however, don't worry – Twitter could be for you. With its 140 character limit and proliferation of acronyms and poor grammar, it's the social networking site of choice for everyone from reality TV stars to professional footballers to nobodies like you. However, the language of texts and social network sites can be confusing to a normally-minded person, so here is a guide to the most frequently used acronyms.

LOL – Leaning On Lamp-post – meaning that the writer may be either Marlene Dietrich or George Formby. Probably best to find out which before embarking on a conversation about ukuleles.

OMG – The lesser-known '80s synth-pop band, Orchestral Manoeuvres in the Garage.

PMSL – Pleasuring Myself Lightly – meaning that the writer finds your message particularly interesting.

LMAO – Let My Auntie Out – a very specific and urgent message.

ROFLMAO – Room's On Fire, Let My Auntie Out – an even more specific and urgent message.

SPEED DATING

Speed dating is a relatively new phenomenon, originating in the United States of America like so many other ridiculous ideas. Men and women take part in what appears to be musical chairs for single people, chatting briefly to one prospective partner before moving swiftly on to another, hence the name. Originally there were three speeds – 45, 78 and 33⅓. Now however, the attention span of the modern young person means that at many events, you have an average of less than 30 seconds to introduce yourself, bond and forge a meaningful relationship. It is therefore vital that you limit your conversation to short, pithy statements containing single syllable words only. If you have a particularly long name you may want to consider having it shortened by deed poll to save vital seconds.

THE FIRST DATE

Once you've finally found your potential Mr or Miss Right, the next step is to arrange a date. But before you do I recommend you take into account the following factors.

WHERE TO GO

Choosing an appropriate venue for your first date can be tricky. Ideally, you want somewhere conducive to relaxed, flowing conversation with just a hint of romance. Generally, it's best to avoid the following: launderettes, post offices, pet shops, underground car parks, landfill sites and ex-partner's homes.

Here are some of my personal recommendations with pros and cons to assist you with your decision:

Bars/Pubs

Pros – A convivial, informal environment which allows you to get to know your date. A little alcohol can help reduce inhibitions to the point where conversation can flow freely.
Cons – A lot of alcohol can reduce inhibitions to the point where your lunch can flow freely.

Restaurants

Pros – A meal in a candlelit French restaurant can be very romantic. It also gives you a focus for the evening in case you and your date struggle to find topics to discuss.
Cons – A meal in a Burger King may not be quite so romantic.

Cinemas

Pros – Going to see a film together takes the pressure off the evening – you don't need to fill the time with idle chit-chat. Sitting in the back row can make you feel like a teenager in love. It also allows for the time-honoured 'arm-round-the-shoulder' routine.

Cons – Your date running up and down the aisles shooting the other cinema-goers with an imaginary space pistol can make you feel like a teenager babysitting your little brother (just one of the many reasons I haven't been to the cinema with Stephen since 1983).

Art Galleries
Pros – They can provide an opportunity to connect on a higher cultural plane.
Cons – Your date running up and down the corridors shooting the other visitors with an imaginary space pistol (we haven't visited an art gallery since 1983 either).

DRESSING FOR A FIRST DATE

First impressions are terribly important so it's vital you strive to make the best one possible by choosing appropriate attire. While I obviously have no idea of the contents of your wardrobe (although if it's anything like mine it can be anything from the latest haute couture to Primark, depending on who Stephen's hidden in there) and am therefore not in a position to advise each and every one of you personally, here are his and hers blanket lists of what not to wear.

Him:
A blanket.
A t-shirt with a slogan – at best they can appear juvenile, such as I'm With Stupid, provocative e.g. Ban the Bomb or downright offensive e.g. any of Stephen's.

A medallion.
Flippers.
An eye patch.
A false beard.
Roller skates.
A tin foil hat.

Her:
Anything that might give him the wrong idea. Which could be anything, really – you know what men are like.

BODY LANGUAGE

Other than your sartorial appearance, how you behave physically is awfully important. Apart from the basics such as sitting up straight and not picking your nose (or your date's), there are countless ways you can affect the outcome of your meeting by the correct use of what body language experts call body language.

Mirroring – this is where someone unconsciously mimics another's physical movements. It occurs when one person is attracted to another and has the subliminal effect of heightening interest in the mirroree – assuming there is such a word, and if there wasn't, there is now. It is easy to replicate this natural reaction by simply copying your date's movements – raising your hand to your face when they raise theirs, crossing your legs when they cross theirs, jumping on the table and removing all your clothes when they remove theirs, etc (although I personally would steer clear of the last one).

Eye contact – when you make prolonged eye contact with your date, you are showing them that you are attracted to them and interested in what they are saying. This can, of course, be difficult if you're naturally shy or you're dating someone like Stephen. I recommend practising at home – stand in front of your bathroom mirror for as long as you can, staring deeply into the reflection of your own eyes until either your vision becomes blurred or the Candyman appears. If either of these occurs, it's probably best to stop for a little while.

Using your date's name – frequent use of your date's name is a strong verbal signal, reinforcing their importance to you. It also helps if you have a poor memory or you're a bit of a slut like my dear friend Mrs Norton. When adopting this strategy, it's vital that you use the correct name and also that you don't giggle if it's a particularly silly name.

Licking your lips provocatively – this can be a very flirtatious act if performed properly. If not, however, it can look like you're fond of Labrador impressions or you've recently been released from a secure psychiatric unit. Either way, I would recommend a fairly robust lipstick (see earlier section – *What Not to Wear On a First Date – Him*).

Make 'em laugh – if you really want to impress your date, make her laugh (note, this only applies to men as most men are intimidated by funny women. And sharks). You can do this in all sorts of ways – making witty observations about fellow diners, relating amusing anecdotes about your boss – but it's important not to go too far. A spinning bow tie or a one-man rendition of *The Importance of Being Earnest* can be inappropriate in the wrong company.

'Accidental' touching – this refers to the brief, seemingly accidental touching of your date, such as grazing their arm with yours or your fingers meeting when reaching for the salt cellar, as opposed to touching your date – or indeed yourself – in a more prolonged and vigorous fashion, which instead of awakening their interest can provoke anything from a slap in the face to a tasering.

Eating – if you're in a restaurant, your choice of meal is terribly important. Be sure to avoid anything too messy or difficult to eat. It can be very off-putting for your date to have to carry on a conversation whilst ignoring the spinach in your teeth or gravy in your hair. Remember the old adage – a moment on the lips, what seems like a lifetime down your cleavage.

CONVERSATION

The real key to a successful first date is conversation. This is how you make that initial emotional contact with someone and turn a virtual stranger into a virtual life partner. Suitable topics of conversation are music, art, films and the weather. Topics of conversation best avoided include phlegm, keyhole surgery, necrophilia and Daniel O'Donnell.

A good way to show that you are interested in your date is

to ask them plenty of questions, although judging the right tone of questioning can be difficult if you're unused to dating – too light a tone can come across as superficial and dull, too heavy can be off-putting to someone you have only just met. Here are a few examples to give you an idea.

Too light – What is your favourite colour?
Just right – What is your favourite film?
Too heavy – What is your favourite sexual position?

Too light – Do you have a family?
Just right – Are you close to your family?
Too heavy – Have you ever had inappropriate feelings about a member of your immediate family?

Too light – Do you know where there's a good greengrocer?
Just right – Do you know where there's a good Italian restaurant?
Too heavy – Do you know where there's a good registry office?

Too light – Can you tell the difference between butter and margarine?
Just right – Can you touch your nose with your tongue?
Too heavy – Can you help me load this sofa into the back of my windowless van?

If you follow this advice, your first date should go swimmingly and before you know it, you'll be exchanging rings and bodily fluids like nobody's business!

But before you book the church, there's one very important

thing to consider – your 'couple name'. This is something that can be overlooked in the romantic whirlwind of courtship but can be crucial to the success of your marriage. For example, my name is Edna, my current husband's is Stephen and so our couple name is Ednaphen, which sounds like some kind of headache pill – and is therefore highly appropriate. Other examples are Paul and Amanda who when couple-named become Panda, which is fairly cute if you like that kind of thing, and my personal favourite is the combination of Stan and Pam – Spam. But I suggest you proceed very carefully as not all couples are so fortunate. Simon and Phyllis become Siphyllis, which is clearly unacceptable as, apart from anything else, it's spelled incorrectly. Other couplings best avoided include Peter and Eunice and Felicity and Horatio.

One final word of caution, dears – no matter how prepared you are, the course of true love doesn't always run smooth, as the following chapter from my forthcoming best-selling auto-biography, *Do We Need To Talk About Stephen?* (an entirely factual account of events and not in any way a complete fantasy influenced by too many years spent reading romantic novels and watching romantic movies on television while waiting for Stephen to return from the pub/bookies/Costa del Sol) illustrates only too well ...

BRIEF ENCOUNTERS

It is a truth universally acknowledged, that a single woman must be in want of a husband in possession of a good fortune. Failing that, his own van.

It all began quite innocently. Every Thursday morning, I took the nine fifteen bus into Spiffing Burberry. I would spend my day nosing blissfully around bookshops, the art gallery and various other establishments, before visiting the cinema, and finally taking tea in the Cuppa Cabana café by the bus station before returning on the six fifty-two to my regular, slightly humdrum life.

Week after week I followed the exact same schedule until one fateful Thursday. A Thursday that would change my life forever. Or for a while, at least.

Everything about the day had been just the same as always. I had stepped out of the café and was about to head for the bus station when I felt something in my eye. I reached up in an attempt to remove it but, before my hand touched my face, I felt another slightly larger, slightly more masculine hand grab my own.

'I'm sorry, allow me . . .'

I stood frozen to the spot, squinting at the large, blurred figure before me as he gently pulled up my eyelid.

'Trust me,' he smiled, 'I'm a doctor,' and in one swift, clinical movement, removed the offending article.

'Just a piece of grit,' he said, beaming broadly as he casually flicked it over his shoulder, 'Easily removed.'

I blinked and looked him up and down. He was tallish, darkish and fairly ordinary-looking. 'Thank you,' I said, shakily. 'Are you an optician?'

'A chiropodist,' he grinned, before adding breezily, 'Well, I must be off – I have a bus to catch. Good day.'

And he was gone.

I thought no more of this curious incident during the days

that followed, or of the quite tall, fairly dark, reasonably good-looking gentleman involved. It never crossed my mind as I lay awake at night or took my thrice-daily stress-relieving baths.

When Thursday finally came around again, the matter had entirely slipped from my consciousness. And so it was with complete and utter surprise that I found myself once more blinking furiously on the step of the Cuppa Cabana in front of the very same gentleman.

'I believe you have something in your eye again,' he said kindly, 'Allow me ...'

The same thing happened the following Thursday. And the Thursday after that.

On the fifth Thursday, I was prepared and before he could grasp my eyelid between his manly thumb and forefinger, I recoiled.

'Sir, why do you keep throwing grit in my eye?' I demanded.

The gentleman blushed slightly. 'Forgive a romantic fool for his clumsy attempt to attract a beautiful lady's attention.'

'No,' I said, and went home.

I didn't go into Spiffing Burberry the next Thursday. Or the next. I was far too busy making cups of tea and taking baths. In truth, the brief encounters of the past weeks had unnerved me somewhat. Who was this irritating, tall, dark, roguishly handsome gentleman who persisted in pursuing me? I wondered whether I ought to inform the police of his behaviour. Instead, however, I resolved to confront him one more time – to tell him to keep his grit to himself and thereby reclaim my precious Thursdays.

When the day arrived, I followed my usual routine other

than in one aspect. For a reason I can't adequately explain, I bought a cup of coffee rather than my usual tea while waiting for the six fifty-two bus home. Actually, I can adequately explain it – the tea in the Cuppa Cabana's terrible. The owner, a slightly vague lady by the name of Ivy Manilow, couldn't make a decent cup of tea if her life depended on it, the poor dear. I don't know why I've been drinking it all these years. Pity, I suppose. But now, something had changed. For some reason I felt different. If only the coffee weren't dreadful too.

Having emptied my cup (into a nearby cactus pot) I placed it on the chipped sombrero-shaped saucer, took a deep breath and made for the door. I had rehearsed this moment countless times over the past few days but my hands were still shaking as I opened the café door and stepped outside. I flinched, blinked hard and rubbed my eye. Then slowly, I lowered my hand. And opened my eye. I could see perfectly. It was entirely grit-free. I frowned and looked around. The street was empty. Not a single tall, dark, devastatingly gorgeous gentleman to be seen. I checked my watch. Six forty-eight. The exact same time I always left the Cuppa Cabana. Had I somehow got the day wrong? I popped back into the café to check the calendar behind Miss Manilow's counter. 1948. Poor dear. But it was definitely Thursday.

As I travelled home, my mind raced. As did the bus. The lady bus driver seemed to be in a terrible hurry for some reason. Why hadn't he been there? What could have happened to him? Perhaps he had been involved in some terrible accident or worse still, lost interest? I sighed in spite of myself – I had to admit I missed his suave, sophisticated, grit-flinging charm. If only there were a way to find him, but how? I didn't even know his name, let alone where to look. In fact, I didn't know anything about him apart from the fact that he was tall, dark and almost god-like in appearance. Or did I? Wait, I did know something. Something that might just enable me to find him …

The following Thursday, I took the nine fifteen bus as usual, I nosed around the bookshop as usual and then I did something unusual …

'Next.'

I stood up gingerly, cast a pained expression in the direction of the receptionist and hobbled towards the door.

Spiffing Burberry was not a large town. It had just one bookshop, one art gallery, one Latin American-themed cafeteria and, according to the telephone directory, one chiropodist. I paused at the door to read the brass plate. So that was his name! I found myself girlishly imagining his surname after my own name and smiled. Somehow, it just sounded right … Edna Chanderpaul.

It was with a heavy heart and a bandaged foot that I trudged along the street that Thursday afternoon. Dr Chanderpaul had been awfully nice and had even lanced my persistent verruca but he wasn't my tall, dark Adonis – not even close. I arrived earlier than usual at the Cuppa Cabana that evening and was forced to wait several minutes before being served while Ivy 'entertained' the other patrons with what the barely legible scrawl on the blackboard described as her Magical Mexican Medley. To be fair to the poor dear, she was almost certainly the best, if not the only one-woman mariachi band in the home counties and that club foot and lazy eye of hers couldn't help.

When she finally finished and managed to locate the counter, I ordered a hot chocolate. Goodness only knew what was happening to me. It was as if I'd suddenly been awakened to the many wondrous possibilities life had to offer – like I'd been living in some kind of flat, monochrome world and all of a sudden my life was now in glorious technicolor. I sat down on my usual seat next to the door (there was no need to go completely crazy), took a sip from my cup and sighed deeply. It was as bad as the coffee.

I was on the verge of throwing caution completely to the wind and catching the six twenty-three, when the café door suddenly blew open and a large body pushed past my chair, almost making me miss the cactus pot with my cup. I looked up at the swarthy, crumpled figure leaning on the counter, gruffly demanding a tequila sunrise and lager chaser. Although I was quite certain I had never seen this objectionable-looking character before, there was something unsettlingly familiar about him. Or his back, at least.

Chiropodist, my foot!

I sank into my seat, lowered the brim of my hat and peered at the figure from behind the inordinately large laminated menu. Seemingly oblivious to my presence, the gentleman – if you could call him that – knocked down his beer and cocktail in two hearty swigs before belching loudly, wiping his chin with his sleeve and exiting sharply.

My mind raced. Was this really the same well-spoken chap I had encountered all those Thursday evenings? It didn't make sense – I had to know more. Without hesitation, I slipped out of the door in pursuit. I was just in time to see his dishevelled figure turn into another building at the end of the street. A few brisk steps took me to its rather dingy front door. Being a lady of considerable refinement, I of course know little of these things but it appeared to be some kind of club – exactly what kind I had no idea. I also have no idea what possessed me at that moment but the next thing I remember doing was pushing open the door and descending a small staircase into a cavern-like room filled with smoke and chatter. As my eyes grew accustomed to the gloom, I noticed what looked like a small stage in the corner of the room on which stood a number of tall, slim microphone stands and a set of drums.

A sudden fear gripped me as I realised this must what young people refer to as a rave. I turned to head back up the stairs but before I reached the first step, the resounding twang of what I could only guess was a guitar filled the room. As if hypnotised by a theatrical illusionist, I turned silently and slowly to see four young mop-headed men standing on the stage. The gentleman I assumed was their lead singer clasped his microphone between long, sturdy fingers and began to sing.

There was no doubt about it – it was him. My mystery grit-flinger. I should have been shocked. I should have been disgusted. I should have turned and walked right out of there. And yet, there was something about him. Gone was the refined, sophisticated gentleman I had almost come to know and in his stead was something very different. Something raw. Something animalistic. Something dangerous. A shiver ran up my spine. Then down my spine. Then around my hipbone. I was transfixed as he yelled into his microphone and strutted before the audience waving his bare, muscular arms in the air.

There was nothing I could do. It was love at seventh sight. I took a seat in a dark corner and just stared. And listened ...

'Thank you, ... ' he yelled as the rapturous applause that attended their first tune finally died down. 'And now, a little song I've just written about a very special lady.'

My heart skipped a beat. Could he possibly mean me?

' ... A lady who came into my life very recently ... on the number nine bus ... '

My heart skipped another beat. He did mean me! I could hardly believe it! I sighed as I gazed at him standing there, so strong and yet so vulnerable, with his bare arms covered in blue tattoos and his fur waistcoat, like a cross between a Smurf and a kitten – he was smitten! I swallowed hard as the first chord struck up and he began to sing ...

> 'I think I'm gonna get off,
> I won't need to pay, yeah,
> The girl that's driving the bus
> Is going my way.
>
> I've got no ticket to ri-hide,
> She's pulling off to the si-hi-hide,
> Think someone's gonna get Fryed,
> But I'm not scared.
>
> She says she'd noticed me there,
> When I rang her bell, yeah,
> I asked 'Can I go all the way?'
> And she answered 'Hell, yeah.'

> She's kinda tickety-boo-hoo,
> She's kinda tickety-boo-hoo-hoo,
> She's kinda tickety-boo
> I guess she'll do.

> I don't know what she does with her tongue,
> I'm worried she'll bite,
> But that is alright by me,
> That thing with the courgette's just plain wrong,
> It doesn't feel right,
> It makes me feel quite queasy.'

My body froze. So, the only reason he kept appearing near the bus station wasn't because he was interested in me at all. I was merely a victim of his silly pranks – an amusing distraction while he waited for his real love – the lady who drove my bus! Suddenly the band's tune took on a melancholy air as my mind began to supply its own lyrics …

> I think I'm going to be sick,
> I found out today, yes,
> That chap who gets on my wick,
> Has started to stray.

> He's got a secret to hi-hide,
> He's taking me for a ri-hi-hide,
> He's got a bit on the side
> And that's not fair.

> I don't know what he sees in that girl,
> She doesn't drink right,
> Stand at the sink right like me,
> He's living in his own little world,
> If he can think that
> I'd let him do that to me!

Before I knew it I was standing back out in the street, my head swimming. I was about to make a move for the bus station when I felt a strong hand grip my shoulder. I swivelled round to see ... him. I tried to speak but I was too upset, too embarrassed to make a noise. I simply stared blankly as he smiled weakly and opened his mouth ...

> 'I think I'd better explain,
> It's the right thing to do, yeah,
> From now, I'm getting the train,
> I'll do it for you.
>
> She's kinda tickety-boo-hoo,
> She's kinda tickety boo-hoo-hoo,
> She's kinda tickety-boo
> But she's not you.'

I blinked hard. It must have been a reflex following all that grit. I took a deep breath and replied coldly ...

> 'I don't know why you're keeping in touch,
> That girl you undressed
> Is of no interest to me.

> I think you've had one lager too much,
> I've my best frown on,
> Why are you down on one knee …?'

The next few minutes are a bit of a blur. The next thing I remember is staring at the sparkling jewel on my finger and then down at my new fiancé, rocking slightly as he sang quietly to himself …

> 'I think I'd better get up,
> I think I might cry, yeah,
> Soon as she signs the pre-nup,
> She'll be Mrs Fry, yeah
>
> I'll take it all in my stri-hide,
> This time there's nowhere to hi-hi-hide
> I'm gonna make her my bride,
> But I'm not scared.
>
> Well, maybe I'm scared,
> Well, maybe I'm scared,
> Well, maybe I'm scared …'

I helped him to his feet as he repeated himself and slowly faded away…

CHAPTER TWO

The Big Day

THE RING

*Please note, this section refers to the choosing, purchase and
giving of the engagement ring, not the Hollywood remake
of the hugely successful horror movie about deceased
Korean girls climbing out of television sets.*

B UYING an engagement ring for your future fiancé can be
a daunting exercise. Should you opt for a traditional or
contemporary design? What stone should you choose?
How much should you spend? How big is her finger? There's
no need to panic but these are all questions you need to
answer in order to ensure the proposal and possible subsequent marriage aren't a complete disaster. But don't fret,
dear, Edna is here to help ...

So, traditional or contemporary? Well, this really depends
on your girlfriend/significant other/whatever you young
people are calling it these days. Is she a traditional or contemporary kind of person? If she likes reading Jane Austen,
listening to Beethoven and playing the lute, she's probably
traditional. If she likes reading Heat magazine, listening to
N'Dubz and playing Grand Theft Auto, she probably leans

more to the contemporary side. Traditional rings tend to be more ornate and often contain clusters of smaller stones, whereas a contemporary design is often simpler and sleeker with just a single stone. Either way, you have a further choice to make – what type of stone?

When picking a stone, you have a myriad of options – rubies, sapphires, emeralds, diamonds and so on. In my opinion, however, nothing says I love you better than something from the *Post-Midnight-What-a-Gem Channel*'s Cubic Zirconium range. But with such a vast array, how on earth can you make a decision? To make things easier reduce your options – you can dismiss anything too large as it can appear a little gaudy, such as napkin rings and swans. You can probably also discount ankle bracelets and toe rings. When choosing a diamond, experts will tell you to be guided by the four Cs – Carat, Clarity, Colour and Cut. When choosing cubic zirconium, if you remember the four Rs – Reduced, Rust-free, Returnable and Round – you won't go far wrong.

Now to answer what can be the most awkward and yet most important question. How much should you spend on an engagement ring? This can depend on a few factors – how romantic you are, your financial situation, and whether you want your partner to say yes or not. The generally accepted rule is you should spend between one and three months' salary – or in Stephen's case, social security payments. Any more could be vulgar and financially crippling, any less could be construed as sarcastic. Fortunately for Stephen, just before he was about to buy my engagement ring he had a rather large win at the 3.15 at Chepstow. Unfortunately for Stephen, I found the betting slip and he had to spend the winnings on my engagement ring instead of jet-ski lessons and a share in a greyhound.

And so we come finally to the issue that has plagued prospective husbands for centuries – size. It's all very well picking out the perfect engagement ring, but it loses its romantic sheen if your fiancé has to wear it on her thumb or through her nose.

So, assuming you wish your proposal to be a wonderful surprise and not a hollow, pre-planned event hinting at a marriage filled with empty predictability, how do you ensure that when you pop the question and place that ring on your loved one's finger, it will make it past the first knuckle? I have to say that my very own Stephen, bless him, came up with an ingenious answer – eventually. Before he had his eureka moment, however, I found my ring finger being thrust variously into a ball of Plasticene, a tub of I Can't Believe It's Not Butter and, on one occasion, a can of baked beans. While most women might have found this all a little confusing, if not downright disturbing, it pretty much fell within the normal parameters of behaviour for Stephen and so I suspected nothing. Finally, after countless unsuccessful attempts, he hit on his master plan.

One Sunday morning, I woke to find my finger in Stephen's mouth. Again, there was nothing especially odd about this – particularly on a Sunday morning – however, when I finally managed to remove it, instead of following his usual routine, he leapt out of bed, pulled on his leather trousers and Batman t-shirt and dashed out of the house, his lips fixed in a small circle. Unfortunately, Stephen had forgotten that the jewellers weren't open on a Sunday and so was forced to spend the next 24 hours with a ridiculous bewildered look on his face. Again, I suspected nothing.

Finally, in case you ladies were feeling left out, there is a recent move towards parity, presumably created by the marketing department of the British jewellery manufacturing industry – Mengagement rings. Call me old-fashioned but I can't help but see this as a disturbing trend – whatever next? Manscara? Misterectomies? Chapstick?

THE PROPOSAL

Asking a loved one, or anyone, to marry you can be a traumatic business – this is why we women generally leave it to the man. I can remember Stephen proposing to me as if it were yesterday – no matter which medication I try. I can still see him now, on that empty, moonlit street, getting up on one knee and uttering those immortal words – 'Edna, my darling. I love you more than anything in the world. Would you do me the enormous honour of consenting to carry me home? You're my best mate, you are.'

Granted, it wasn't a conventional proposal (like so many men, Stephen finds it difficult to express himself where matters of the heart are involved – or after 12 pints of Stella) but I knew exactly what he meant, the dear romantic soul. Having said that, it still came as a bit of a surprise, as up to that point the most romantic question he'd asked me was 'have you done with those chips?'. In fact, I think Stephen even surprised himself, feigning complete ignorance the following morning – he's such a tease. He even claimed he hadn't bought me an engagement ring, the big silly. As it turned out, he hadn't, but a girl can't have everything and I knew he would get me one as soon as he could afford it. For now, our love was enough. For now …

Of course, there are additional pressures should you and your partner happen to be a celebrity couple like Stephen and myself (although admittedly, I'm the only actual celebrity – Stephen's just my trophy husband. Not as in the World Cup or Wimbledon, you understand – more like one of those plastic Oscars you can purchase from fancy dress shops). Television news programmes still regularly replay the sadly prophetic words spoken by HRH Prince Charles on the occasion of his first engagement. When asked 'Do you love Diana?' his famous, somewhat hesitant response was 'Of course … whatever love is'.

By contrast, Stephen was far more forthright at our engagement party when somebody asked him 'Do you love Edna?'.

'Of course!' he announced, wildly waving a bottle of champagne in the air, ' … whoever Edna is.'

THE WEDDING

Unless you're very careful, the cost of your big day can run to hundreds of pounds – money which could be better spent on a three-piece suite or Sky Plus. And here we come to the thorny issue of who pays for it all. Traditionally, it was the bride's father's responsibility to cover the cost of the wedding but nowadays, with spiralling costs, it's more likely that it will be shared between both sets of parents, either by splitting everything equally or by one pair paying for the reception, photographer, dress etc and the other paying for the honeymoon. This second option is, however, a little unfair as whoever pays for the reception, flowers etc has the opportunity to enjoy them whereas very few couples tend to take either the bride or groom's parents with them on their honeymoon.

One option available to minor celebrity couples is to have a popular gossip magazine pay for their wedding, allowing them a lavish occasion at no expense plus additional much-needed publicity. Sadly, this option isn't open to most couples although a little initiative can bring you similar advantages. The bride, for example, could negotiate a discount by offering to wear a wedding dress emblazoned with the name of the dress shop. At our own wedding, Stephen was sponsored by Kevin's kebab van and the Kashmiri Palace – and our honeymoon was paid for by a company called Candid Camera Midnight Movies Ltd, although I've still no idea what they got out of it.

A further option for those operating on a tight budget is to take out one of these new wedding day loans advertised on daytime television, but I recommend exercising extreme caution – the interest rate can be excessive and if you fail to pay the amount back within the allotted time, they will have no hesitation in taking your dress, ring and head bridesmaid as collateral.

WHERE TO GET MARRIED

These days, there are countless options open to the bride and groom other than the traditional church or registry office — couples can tie the knot while sky-diving, snorkelling and competing in the 400 metres hurdles. They can get married in a hotel, on the beach, on a football pitch (provided a match isn't taking place or they're really quick), even their own front room. They can even have a romantic movie-themed wedding such as *An Officer and a Gentleman*, *Gone with the Wind* and *Reservoir Dogs*. Being a thoroughly modern open-minded woman, I have no objections to such a frivolous approach to what should be the most significant day of your life. Stephen, however, is far more conservative. When we got married, he insisted on nothing less than the full traditional Elvis drive-thru wedding. Sadly, his window cleaner's salary didn't run to two tickets to Vegas, so he went on his own and we were married in the Aberystwyth Shakin' Stevens Chapel of Love a few months later.

It was a truly magical occasion. We walked down the aisle to the strains of *This Ole House* and when we reached the altar, the fully-quiffed vicar emerged from behind a green door in his drainpipe trousers and winkle-pickers. Of course, it wasn't the real Shaky — he was one of the ushers — but his frantic hip action and profuse sweating made the event truly rock 'n' roll, in every sense of the word. Well, the one sense of the word. Or words.

WHO TO MARRY

See Chapter One.

THE INVITATION

Once you have decided on a date, venue and potential spouse, the next stage is to send out the invitations (N B if you're planning to elope, skip this step to avoid any unnecessary awkwardness). Of course, in order to do this, you must first draw up a list of wedding guests. If you are working to a tight budget, it's important to be realistic. I would recommend limiting yourselves to immediate family and close personal friends – Elton John and Lady Gaga don't come cheap.

Invitations come in all shapes and sizes – you can splash out on tailor-made embossed designs or simply buy a pack from your newsagent. I wrote ours on the back of Stephen's betting slips. Whatever you do, don't forget to ask them for an R S V P (Really Strong Vodka, Please).

THE DRESS

Never mind all the pomp and ceremony, the I dos and the I-won't-if-you-don't-minds, the one thing everyone will be talking about before, during and after your wedding will be the dress – 'What will it be like?', 'How much did it cost?' and 'How much?!?'.

The wedding dress is the single most important and, in all

probability, expensive item of clothing a woman will ever wear. Especially when you consider that, unless she's a bridal wear model or psychologically disturbed, she'll only wear it the once. Which all adds to the not inconsiderable pressure of choosing the right one. Off the shoulder or not? Too much cleavage or too little? Should you have a veil? A train? A matching handbag?

And what colour should it be? Traditionally, the wedding dress was always white, reflecting the virginal nature of the bride. Nowadays, in our more permissive society, such a state can no longer be guaranteed. Of course I wore white for my wedding (it matched the baby) but today there are a whole host of possibilities – ivory, cream, fluorescent pink. Before making this crucial decision, I recommend asking for a small sample piece of material in each colour to match against your skin. If your dress shop or catalogue doesn't offer this service, pop into B&Q and buy the corresponding match pots (remember also to purchase some thinner to remove the paint from your skin afterwards).

Once you have settled on a dress colour, it's time to pick a design. This can be easier said than done as not all women share my instinctive understanding of haute couture. Don't worry, dears – I'm here to help. Firstly, you want a style that will suit your body shape. Again, not many women share my perfect hourglass figure so it's vital you choose a dress tailored to make the most – or least – of whatever nature has provided you with. The slimmer lady can cope with a close-fitting, simple design whereas with the fuller figure, the more bows, ruffles and feathers the better, provided you can still fit down the aisle.

The length of the dress is another important aspect to think about. If the lady concerned is taller than average she should go for a relatively longer cut (unless she's Mrs Norton). If she's shorter in stature then the opposite. Being a taller lady myself (Stephen refers to me as his Spamazon), I know only too well the importance of the right length of garment although one shouldn't go too long at the risk of appearing overly ostentatious. Also try to avoid what I call 'the meringue effect' in which the bride catches her heel in the hem and ends up in the raspberry pavlova.

And remember! It's essential that your husband-to-be doesn't see the dress before the wedding. If he does, he might go online and find out how much it cost before it's too late.

GROOMWEAR

By contrast, the task of the groom is much easier as he only has to decide where to buy his suit and even this decision is often made for him by his budget – Hugo Boss, Top Man or Suits 'R' Us. There are options, however, to add a little flair – or flares, in Stephen's case. Cravats, cufflinks and cummerbunds are just some funny words beginning with C.

A wedding provides a chance for the groom to celebrate his ancestry. If he is of Scottish descent, he can opt for a kilt in his family tartan. Stephen has Irish roots so he wore a shamrock in his buttonhole and his most Guinness-stained jeans.

One extra little luxury a groom can indulge in prior to the wedding is a professional shave. This doesn't come cheaply but I know Stephen thoroughly enjoyed it and by all accounts so did the professional lady he shaved.

THE GIFT LIST

Whatever you do, make sure you provide all of your guests with a list of gifts you would like. Many large department stores offer this service which ensures you don't end up with eight teapots (six should be enough for anyone). On the list, you can put a range of items varying in price from hideously expensive for closer and richer relatives to just a couple of pounds for distant relatives and cheapskates. To ensure we received gifts we both really wanted, Stephen and I drew up two lists – mine from British Home Stores and his, Bargain Booze.

STAG AND HEN NIGHTS

Otherwise known as Bachelor and Bachelorette parties, Stag and Hen nights have become as integral a part of the wedding as the reception, the photographs and, to an extent, the service. Over the years they have become more and more elaborate with many grooms now favouring an entire weekend of debauchery. As I recall, Stephen had a stag decade.

HEN DOS AND DON'TS

In years gone by, a bride-to-be's hen night was a thoroughly respectable affair. While her future husband spent half the night chained to a parking meter minus his trousers after spending the other half carousing with dancing ladies of dubious repute minus his trousers, she was far more likely to be found at her mother's home with a handful of close female friends and relatives engaging in far more genteel pursuits such as drinking tea and practising writing her married name.

These days, however, things have taken a considerable turn for the worse. The so-called modern woman is no longer satisfied with such perfectly agreeable behaviour – she is far more likely to be found careering drunkenly from bar to bar dressed in nothing but an L plate and a g-string and, if anything, behaves even worse on her hen night.

As if this type of display weren't bad enough, high street stores have spotted a money-making opportunity and the modern bride-and bridesmaids-to-be can now be seen stumbling around in all manner of ridiculous, revealing outfits – sexy nurses, sexy devils, sexy police officers, sexy sewage workers – the list is endless. In comparison, the men appear drab and inconsequential – the opposite of the animal kingdom where it is generally the females who are the drab ones and the males wearing the sexy nurse costumes.

It's my firm belief that all this new-found pre-wedding equality has left today's woman floundering, pressured into atypical behaviour due to this new social convention. To assist you poor, confused young ladies facing these choppy waters, I've provided a few simple don'ts and dos to help steer you safely through and keep your reputation and wedding plans intact.

Don't

... drink alcohol. It lowers the inhibitions and you certainly don't want to be doing that now, do you? Excessive consumption can make you behave in a manner unbefitting a young lady and lead you to make questionable decisions such as drinking a rack of exotically flavoured vodka shots instead of a nice glass of sparkling water, taking an unlicensed mini-cab home instead of a council-registered taxi or engaging in a three-in-a-bed romp with your fiancé's brother and best friend instead of not engaging in a three-in-a-bed romp with your fiancé's brother and best friend.

... under any circumstances, allow your friends to book any unsolicited entertainment for the evening such as a male stripper or gorillagram (essentially a slightly hairier male stripper). Apart from the excruciating embarrassment the bride-to-be can feel whilst reluctantly engaging in lewd acts such as spanking and simulated banana consumption (or so I'm led to believe), there can be further complications should the gorillagram turn out to be the poor unfortunate girl's future husband who somehow failed to mention his additional part-time career, preferring to tell her he was down the Dog & Duck every week-night, playing darts with his mates when he should have been at home helping her look after her six or seven children. For example.

Do

... wrap up snugly in a nice, robust jumper – ideally one with a kitten or other domestic pet on the front. Although many weddings, and consequently the associated hen nights, take place in the spring and summer it is best not to take any chances. To avoid finding yourself with a dose of influenza on your 'big' day, I also recommend you wear a thick pair of woollen tights, preferably brown or grey, to discourage any unwanted bacterial visits to your nether regions. Other items worth serious consideration are the following – a pair of mittens and a balaclava (if you don't own a balaclava, a paper bag is an acceptable alternative). I find it's also a good idea to avoid over-use of cosmetics such as foundation, blusher, mascara and lipstick – it only encourages the poor dears. I know only too well the curse of being irresistible to the opposite sex. My face may not have launched a thousand ships but it did once tip over a rowing boat.

… above all, maintain a sense of decorum. Remember, you are not only representing your family but you are an ambassador for the whole of womankind. Every single one of your actions has the potential to undo centuries of female social evolution. The 21st century woman only has the freedom to behave how she likes because of the blood, sweat and toil of women like Emmeline Pankhurst and the suffragettes. Thanks to their unremitting bravery and dedication, you are now able to vote, to walk across uncovered puddles, to attend mixed gender public functions without fainting and drink beer from a pint glass without fear of electric shock treatment. Remember, when you head out to celebrate your impending nuptials you carry the weight of the past and the hopes and dreams of womankind on your shoulders. But above all, have a nice time.

STAG DOS AND DON'TS

Just don't. Whatever it is.

THE SERVICE

In many ways, the service can be seen as the most important part of the wedding day – there's the music, the flowers and a chance for a break from all that standing around making small talk with relatives you've never heard of or thought had died. And as if all this weren't enough, there are the vows. When a bride and groom stand at the altar before their family and friends, they are declaring their love to the world and promising to dedicate the rest of their lives to each other. It can be a very solemn and meaningful moment – but it needn't be. Stephen and I wrote our own vows in order to lighten the mood for ourselves and the congregation. Mine was a beautiful, uplifting, hour-long evocation of romance, passion and joy, quoting Keats, Wordsworth and Shelley. Stephen's was a string of mother-in-law jokes.

THE FLOWERS

Another important consideration for your big day is the flowers. As well as floral displays for the church or wherever you are marrying, there's the all-important bridal bouquet. This is a crucial aspect not only of the bride's apparel but carries with it a further significance as, according to tradition, whoever catches the bouquet after she tosses it into the air at the end of the ceremony will be the next to marry. This can result in quite a hubbub as eager bridesmaids compete for the portentous foliage and the occasional severe injury, as was the case at my own wedding. On reflection, I probably should have had a regular bouquet rather than a yukka plant.

MISCELLANEOUS

Depending on the size of the congregation, you may also wish to choose a few ushers. Their job is to stand at the entrance of the church or registry office, hand out the orders of service and direct members of the bride's and groom's families to the appropriate side of the aisle. Of course, it doesn't really matter where anyone sits – it's just useful to have jobs to give to those too unreliable or stupid to be best man.

In addition to the common traditions, some couples choose to celebrate their love in a more exuberant fashion, releasing a flock of doves during the ceremony. In a similar display, when we got married, Stephen released several of his pigeons into the air. Unfortunately, he hadn't taken into account the vicar's ornithophobia or the fact that they were homing pigeons and the ensuing scenes, as they flew as one into the eves before returning to the altar time and time again, were reminiscent of the more distressing scenes from Alfred Hitchcock's *The Birds*.

AFTER THE SERVICE

The Photographs

Your wedding photographs are a lasting memory of what, for some people, is the most important day of your life and should not be taken lightly. Or with the lens cap on. In this digital age, couples have a number of ways of recording their 'special' day. One popular choice is the wedding video. In the past, these were basic affairs, often shot by an enthusiastic uncle and containing little more than a sequence of blurred, inaudible images (which, to be fair, is pretty much how Stephen remembers our wedding anyway). These days, however, modern technology means that even the most incompetent cameraman can produce an epic worthy of Richard Curtis or Quentin Tarantino. Crystal-clear scenes with perfect sound can be edited with the latest software to produce a delightful record of events with a Celine Dion soundtrack and all kinds of flashy visual effects. In fact, technology has moved on so far that Stephen has even suggested we renew our vows so that he can have a 3D High-definition video with CGI fireworks and a giant monkey-robot.

If, however, your budget doesn't run to such extravagances, don't worry. Modern CCTV cameras can provide relatively un-grainy footage, as long as you're happy to get married on a traffic island or in a branch of WH Smith. Fortunately for me and Stephen, the Shakin' Stevens Chapel of Love was equipped with what for its time was relatively sophisticated recording equipment, due to one of its previous incarnations as a secure home for sexual offenders.

The Reception

While your choice of where to get married is important, it pales into insignificance compared to your choice of where to hold the wedding reception. These days, countless different types and styles of venue are available, from the traditional country hotel to the less traditional lap-dance club. There are many things to consider before making a booking – how many guests will be attending, what budget are you working with and do they do those funny little pink things? Things were so much easier in our day – it was either the Wimpy or, if your family had a bit of money, a Berni Inn.

Once you've made your decision you need to draw up a seating plan, which can be rather more complicated than it sounds, depending on the internal politics of your family. You don't want to make the kind of social faux pas that could result in the embarrassment of being seated at a table full of ex-girlfriends as in *Four Weddings and a Funeral*, or on a table full of monkeys as in *The Jungle Book*. Traditionally, the bride, groom, their parents, best man, chief bridesmaid and cake are seated at the top table but the rest is pretty much up to you. For me, it was relatively simple – my friends and family inside, Stephen's outside.

Entertainment

After the meal, the speeches and the reading out of messages from those unable to attend owing to illness, geography or having something better to do, it's customary to have some form of entertainment, most commonly a disco or band rather than a ventriloquist, as I kept telling Stephen. This gives female guests the opportunity to let their hair down in a tight circle round a pile of handbags, small children to injure themselves and males over the age of 40 to appear on YouTube.

If you book a disco, make sure you check the disc jockey's play list. Ideally, you should be aiming for a light, family-friendly pop assortment including such perennial wedding favourites as *Dancing Queen*, *Build Me Up Buttercup* and *Oops Upside Your Head*, rather than gangster rap or thrash metal. If live music is your preference but your budget is limited, there are any number of relatively inexpensive tribute bands that will guarantee to get your guests' toes tapping and groins thrusting. Stephen's favourites are Earth, Wind and Frank, Nearvana and I Can't Believe It's Not Emerson, Lake and Palmer.

The Cake

The true star of any wedding reception is the cake. It should stand proudly on the top table, a resplendent icing-covered monument to your hopes and dreams. And standing atop this marzipan monolith, a tiny bride and groom, or in our case a subbuteo player and a cocktail stirrer.

The traditional wedding cake, a sturdy fruit cake designed to last decades, has, in recent years, given way to a number of more edible variations including chocolate fudge cake, éclair pyramids and even bizarre meringue-based structures. The following recipe has been in my family for generations – it was handed down to me by my mother, who in turn was given it by her mother, who was given it by her mother, who copied it out of a book.

WEDDING CAKE RECIPE

INGREDIENTS

800 grams of flour

Half a dozen eggs

Two cups of dried fruit

The zest of three oranges

One cup of understanding

Two spoonfuls of love

A gallon of patience

A dash of forgiveness

A hint of desperation

A handful of crushed dreams

150 grams of I Can't Believe It's Not Better

A bag of nerves, grated

One big disappointment (bitter)

METHOD

Mix ingredients together in a large, empty container for several years until any zest has completely disappeared. Place in an un-preheated oven, together with your head, for as long as it takes.

SERVES: you right.

You should have listened to your mother.

Alternatively, get a nice Victoria sponge from the Co-op.

Of course, your wedding guests can't just eat cake – they're not animals, or Stephen. You must make sure all tastes are catered for. Thankfully, the traditional wedding cheese and pineapple hedgehog covers all bases, providing sustenance for those who favour sweet and savoury, and woodland creatures. Another option guaranteed to please is that king of party platters, the prawn ring. (For wedding parties of 50 or more, simply scale up – a cheese and pineapple hog and a dolphin ring should cover it).

If you're looking for that wow factor, and budget will allow, one thing certain to impress your guests is an ice sculpture. Giant swans and unicorns can often be found adorning the dinner tables of the rich and famous but they needn't cost the earth – if you or your partner has an artistic bent, why not make your own? All you need is a chisel, a hammer and a block of ice. Any fool could do it. Or almost any. Sadly, Stephen's attempt to recreate the Virgin Mary ended up looking more like the abominable snowman once he'd finished with his chainsaw. Nevertheless, it proved a talking point, particularly among the paramedics who treated several guests for shock and my great aunt and her sister for hypothermia after it collapsed on their table during the toast.

A safer alternative but no less impressive and more (intentionally) interactive is my personal favourite – the Gravy Fountain. Just imagine the delight on your guests' faces as they crowd round this magnificent structure, eagerly thrusting their skewered sausages, sprouts and lumps of mashed potato into a never-ending stream of mouth-watering, meaty nectar.

The Best Man's Speech

If there's one element of the wedding reception of which I
don't entirely approve, it's the so-called 'best' man's speech.
Often vulgar, frequently embarrassing and almost always
tasteless, Stephen naturally loves them. Personally, I don't see
the need to humiliate and belittle the groom in front of his
entire family. I prefer to wait until the privacy of the honeymoon. It wouldn't be so bad if the 'best' man were an
engaging, witty raconteur along the lines of Peter Ustinov or
that nice Mr Palin. Sadly, more often than not, he's some
semi-literate mate from the pub darts team whose idea of wit
is to pull out his trouser pockets, undo his flies and stand
there wiggling and dangling for all to see. This may raise
laughs from those of a baser nature, but I assure you any
respectable guest would do their best to ignore the elephant
in the room.

The First Dance

One of the more romantic wedding reception traditions is the
first dance, when the newlyweds tentatively take to the floor
to share a few touching moments shuffling awkwardly to
'their song' before imploring the rest of the guests to join
them. This does, however, rely on the couple having 'a song'.
Often it will be the tune they first danced to or one that was
playing in the restaurant where they shared their first romantic dinner. It will be a song both partners love, one that will
instantly fill their heads with memories and their hearts with
love. This isn't always the case, however, especially with couples who have wildly different musical tastes, like me and
Stephen, but never fear, dears – if this sounds like you, there

is a solution. All you need is a friendly disc jockey with a dual turntable and your problem is solved. It's a relatively simple task for him to combine both of your favourite songs into one seamless blend – or mash-up, as I believe the young people call it. I'll never forget the look on everyone's faces as Stephen and I took a turn on the dance floor to the strains of *Everything I Do, I Do It For Puff the Magic Dragon*.

THE WEDDING NIGHT

In days long gone, a crowd of ruddy-faced villagers would gather beneath the window as bride and groom consummated their nuptials, whooping and cheering as the groom would wave a blood-soaked post-coital sheet in the night air to indicate he had successfully relieved his new wife of her virginity. These days, the wedding night is rather more subdued due to the lack of virgins and ruddy-faced villagers. That isn't to say it always runs smoothly. Should you chose to spend your wedding night in a hotel, for example, it's absolutely vital that you reveal your room number to no-one; otherwise you may find yourself spending the night accompanied by a chorus of drunken guests or a sheep – something no self-respecting bride should be doing for at least the first few months of her married life.

THE HONEYMOON

While my own 'big' day may not have been exactly what I would have wished for, it could have been worse. If we had been getting married now, no doubt Stephen would have wanted one of these 'Big Fat Gypsy Weddings' you see on television, although I suppose we did have something of a big fat gypsy honeymoon, what with the bare-knuckle boxing, semi-naked bridesmaids and reality TV crew.

These days, couples expect far more from a honeymoon. It is, after all, the start of your married life – you may as well enjoy the first couple of weeks. Honeymoon destinations are many and varied. Whereas Stephen and I were more than happy with a week's self-catering in Llandudno, modern newly-weds can be found celebrating their nuptials in every corner of the globe, busy snowboarding, snorkelling, white water rafting or whatever young people call the marital act these days. But no matter where you go or what you get up to, the important thing is that you have this transitional period of adjustment between the joyous, thrilling, romantic roller-coaster-ride of the wedding and the interminable decades of marriage ahead.

DID YOU KNOW?

(from Vaguelytruepedia.com) The word 'honeymoon' was originally spelled 'hunnymoon' and first featured in A. A. Milne's *Winnie the Pooh*, in which Pooh sets out one night to trap the mythical heffalump, using a jar of honey as bait. Unfortunately, things don't go to plan and the bear of little brain ends up with his head stuck in the jar, wailing mournfully beneath the moon. This tradition continues, for while newlyweds rarely get any part of their anatomies trapped in a jar nowadays, a great deal of howling at the moon still occurs (interestingly, the phrase 'honey-pot' to describe a woman hired to entice a married man into adultery also has its origin in this book, in the chapter *'In Which Pooh Gets 100 Acre Wood'*).

CHAPTER THREE

The Way To A Man's (or Woman's) Heart

T HEY SAY that the way to a man's heart is through his stomach, and I know this all too well. In spite of my countless other attributes (my loving and patient nature, my creativity, my extreme intelligence, that thing I do with my thumb) I am under no illusion as to why Stephen married me – for my cooking. Like all men, he is never happier than when his stomach is full (apart from our Sunday mornings) and I consider it my primary wifely duty to fill it. I realise it may be unfashionable to make such a statement in this day and age but that doesn't make it any less true. And in turn it makes me happy too. I get a warm feeling inside watching him lying, belching on the sofa after one of my Cordon Bleu meals. The grin on his lips, the faraway look in his eyes, the inability to jump on me unexpectedly and demand his conjugal rights. Of course, I wouldn't expect you to be able to even approach the lowest level of my culinary mountain but I am contractually obliged to include a number of my legendary recipes in this book so here are a few of the less ambitious ones.

BREAKFAST

Nutritionists say that breakfast is the most important meal of the day, and I agree wholeheartedly. Without a good solid breakfast to start his day, Stephen would still be lying in bed winking and rubbing his nipples at lunchtime.

Breakfasts vary wildly from country to country. In the United States, pancakes with maple syrup are the norm, in Scotland they like nothing better than a smoked kipper and glass of Buckfast, whereas much of Europe favours the continental breakfast – a selection of breads, cheeses and cold cuts of meat. Of course none of these impostors can truly compare with the Full English Breakfast – the name itself even tells you how you'll feel after you've eaten it. English food has an undeserved reputation around the world. In fact, the country has produced a great many of the world's finest chefs including, of course, myself. To prove my point, here is my own mouth-watering version of that king of breakfasts, the Full English, featuring only the finest, locally-sourced ingredients (Asda, mostly).

EDNA'S ALL-ENGLISH FRY-UP

Pour four tablespoons of olive oil into a frying pan and place over a low heat. Add the following ingredients –

Six rashers of Danish bacon
Three sausages (any kind will do – bratwurst, knockwurst, Dutch smoked)
200g mushrooms (Portabella or Shiitake)
100g Sauerkraut
Two guavas
250g Cheerios
300g butter popcorn

Increase the heat, stirring slowly until the ingredients have browned, melted or popped. Serve on a large plate with Dijon mustard, puttanesca sauce and a round of strawberry Pop Tarts and there you have my All-English Fry-Up.

BRUNCH

I can't say I approve of this transatlantic snack midway between breakfast and lunch. I much prefer the British term 'elevenses'. Or 'tenses'. Or ideally, both. And what better way to enjoy this mid-morning break than with a packet of HobNobs and a lovely cup of tea. But not so fast, dears. Before you go racing to the kettle read on a little further. After all, if a job's worth doing, it's worth doing my way...

HOW TO MAKE THE PERFECT CUPPA

One crucial marital skill that has been sadly neglected over recent years is the art of making a good cup of tea. So many marriages have floundered as a result of a poorly brewed cuppa for without this seemingly humble act, the wife has no reason to disappear to the kitchen every half hour and nothing to calm her frayed nerves apart from hard liquor. Of course, the two needn't be mutually exclusive – after all, what do you get when you put the words cuppa and tipple together? Couple! Sort of.

Anyway, in order that your marriage doesn't fail due to your inadequate tea-making skills, here's my foolproof method for making the perfect cuppa, worth the price of this book alone. Boy George famously said a cup of tea is better than you-know-what. I'm not sure about that but it certainly takes longer.

WHAT YOU NEED:
A box of good old traditional tea-bags (proper square ones – I don't hold with those new-fangled round and pyramid-shaped ones). You will find so-called experts extolling the virtues of loose tea but, to my mind, anything that can be used for occult purposes should be avoided.
A kettle.
Some water (tap or bottled – preferably still, not sparkling).
A teapot. Some people prefer to make their tea in the cup or mug. It's a free country, of course, and I'm nothing if not

open-minded, but these people are the spawn of Satan and should be made to walk the streets ringing a bell. To make a truly drinkable cup of tea you need a good, sturdy teapot. Not just any old pot, mind – the shape is absolutely crucial to allow the flavour to circulate properly. I would recommend one in the shape of a chicken or thatched cottage.

A cup. Again, some philistines prefer to take their tea from a mug but it's not called a mugga, is it, dears?

Sugar (lumps or granulated)

Milk (liquid)

METHOD

Step 1

Decide how many tea bags to use. This can be a daunting proposition for the novice but it's second nature to a seasoned tea-bagger such as myself. If you prefer a weak brew, one should be sufficient, if you prefer your tea stronger, use two or three. If your husband has just come home from the pub with a traffic cone on his head and another tattoo, I'd recommend at least half a dozen. Place the tea bags into your teapot. Congratulations, dear – you've begun your journey to tea heaven!

Step 2

Make sure the water is the correct temperature. This is a highly specialised skill, requiring years of practice to perfect, so I'll walk you through it slowly…

First, fill your kettle, making sure it doesn't overflow.

Second, plug the kettle into the mains socket, ensuring the flex remains attached to the kettle.

Third, wait and watch (don't worry about the old adage that

a watched pot never boils – a watched kettle always boils, provided you have carried out steps one and two correctly).

Fourth, when the kettle switches itself off, the water has
reached the correct temperature. Pour immediately into your
teapot, making sure not to spill any or leave to cool for several
hours first (this is the fifth instruction, by the way, but I'm sure
you wouldn't want to me to patronise you, now would you,
dear?).

Step 3

Allow the tea to infuse for three minutes, or two if you're
really gasping. Pour the infusion from the teapot into your cup.
Replace teapot lid. Add milk and sugar to taste. Remove tea bag
and drink.

Step 4

Repeat every 15 minutes until bedtime or your husband finally
goes back to the pub.

LUNCH

Spending lunchtime together is a rare event for a modern
couple such as Stephen and myself. More often than not, I
lunch alone at home while he's out on his window cleaning
round or taxi shift, or round at number 38 with you-know-
who. However, in order to help him keep up his strength for
whichever activity he's engaged in, I insist on providing him
with a nutritional, balanced packed lunch, the heart of which
is that king of convenience foods – the sandwich.

There are countless different types of sandwich, from the

humble cheese to the regal cucumber to the elaborate intes-tine-challenging creations of New York delicatessens. Some are even abbreviated – the bacon, lettuce and tomato is known throughout the world simply as the BLT. You can buy sand-wiches from supermarkets, fast food outlets, corner shops and even 24 hour garages (between the car fresheners and the peat). They come in all shapes and sizes with all kinds of fill-ings on every kind of bread. However, as far as I'm concerned, you can't beat a good old-fashioned home made sandwich. And Stephen agrees. You should see the look on his face when he opens up his little Tupperware box to see what it contains that day – it makes all the effort worthwhile. Of course, those who don't know my husband as well as I do might mistake it for a look of disgust, even fear, but I know better. Those wide eyes, bare teeth and rigid cheeks say just one thing to me – love.

As in so many other areas of married life, the secret of suc-cessful sandwiches is variety. Never let your partner know what's coming – that way they can never get bored. Over the years, Stephen's been treated to everything from my prize-winning Egg and Banana to my Walnut, Tuna and Falafel – or, as Stephen calls it, WTF. While some of my mouth-watering creations may seem a little ambitious, there are a number which even the relative sandwich novice can attempt with a fair degree of confidence. One such sandwich is my own spe-cial Club Sandwich. While, no doubt, you will have heard of the Club Sandwich (a rather bland concoction with chicken, bacon, mayonnaise etc), did you know that this is merely one of an entire range? This includes, among others, the Garrick Club Sandwich, the Caravan Club Sandwich, the Culture

Club Sandwich, the Club 18–30 Sandwich (technically not
an item of food) and the Fight Club Sandwich – although I'm
afraid I can't talk about the last one.

My own particular version of this ubiquitous creation is a
hearty, filling and generally digestible addition to the range,
designed to keep even the laziest individual going whether
he wants to or not.

EDNA'S WORKING MEN'S
CLUB SANDWICH

Step 1

First, choose your bread. Now, this isn't as easy as it sounds,
dears. A brief visit to any supermarket will reveal not only
aisles full of desperate single people but also a whole host of
different types of bread – white, brown, beige, whole wheat,
half wheat, half-baked, wholemeal, oatmeal, goatmeal,
granary, nunnery, thick-sliced, thin-sliced, medium-sliced,
unsliced, farmhouse, warehouse, whorehouse, dormouse,
doorstep, quickstep, wraps, baps, bagels, beagles, baguettes,
muffins, crumpets, flatbread, fatbread, cornbread, crisp
bread, lava bread, loofah bread, rice bread, rye bread, soda
bread, cider bread, potato bread, tomato bread, ciabatta bread
etc etc etc – honestly, it's enough to leave your head spinning
– or is that the cooking sherry? Anyway, to keep things simple, I would recommend you use a plain thick-sliced white
loaf.

Step 2

Next you need some kind of spread to keep your sandwich moist – again, keep it simple. As far as I'm concerned (and you should be too), you can't beat good old-fashioned I Can't Believe It's Not Butter. Some people maintain that butter tastes exactly the same but I'm not convinced. Spread two slices of bread evenly on one side. Congratulations – you're well on the way to making your first truly delicious (or, at least, edible) sandwich!

Step 3

First take a deep breath because you have reached the most exciting part of the entire sandwich creation process – The Filling. Or in this case, Fillings – because this is not just any simple sandwich (don't panic, dears, I'm here to help you – just keep a tight hold of my apron strings and you won't get lost). The following is a list of all the things you will need in order to create a perfect Working Men's Club Sandwich.

INGREDIENTS
Scotch Egg
Pork Pie
Pickled Onions – 2
Cheese and Onion Crisps – 35 g

Pork Scratchings – 25 g
Black Forest Gateau – one large slice
Carling lager – two pints

Once you are sure you have all the ingredients, place them carefully one by one into your food processor and press the 'on' button. Once the mixture has reached the required consistency (this may take some time), pour it evenly across one of the slices of bread, using a small teaspoon to remove any unwanted lumps such as bits of crisp packet or glass.

Step 4
Carefully place the other slice of bread, I Can't Believe It's Not Butter-side-down on top of the covered slice and press firmly. Cut into triangles with a knife or, failing that, a power saw, place lovingly into your partner's lunchbox and just wait until you see that look on their face!

❖

HANDY HINT – if you have any loose bricks or roofing tiles, why not make use of any remaining mixture? Waste not, want not, dears!

DINNER

There's nothing more romantic than a couple sharing a delicious candlelit meal in their own home – but how many of us get the opportunity? There's the food-buying, the cooking, the napkin-folding, the candle-lighting and the television switching off – a modern husband or wife simply doesn't have the time or energy for such an undertaking. Well, dears, this is where I come in. Or came in, because not that long ago I ran my very own one-woman catering company providing bespoke romantic dinners for the culinarily-challenged. It was at a time when I felt I needed a more meaningful role in life – and a new hat. I would love to tell you that it was a roaring success but sadly the business folded after just one meal. But what a meal it was ...

I was sitting in the Cuppa Cabana, contemplating life and my dubious-looking cappuccino, when a gentleman asked if he might join me. He informed me that his name was Tom and he was a barista. Presumably poor dear Miss Manilow had finally taken someone on to cover for her during her 'Mariachi moments'. I was briefly concerned, especially when he said he knew all about me and my 'legendary culinary prowess', but his intentions soon became clear. He had heard about my new business venture and was keen for me to provide a romantic dinner for him and his lovely wife Selina that weekend. I said yes, of course. My first booking – I was thrilled! He gave me her name and their address but, before I had the opportunity to quiz him about his wife in order to tailor my meal to her tastes, his mobile phone rang and he was forced to leave. Some urgent legal matter he needed to deal with, apparently – something to do with Miss Manilow's 'special' Colombian blend, no doubt.

And so Saturday evening arrived, as did the Live and Let Dine van at the couple's residence. And what a lovely place it was – clearly the Cuppa Cabana paid its staff considerably more than the average café. After helping me unload several boxes from Stephen's van, the gentleman led me to the kitchen before rejoining his wife. As I unpacked the ingredients, I had a fleeting moment of panic. Not like me at all, but I was keen that my new venture should get off to a good start and I knew nothing about this man's wife apart from her name, Selina Moody-Stuart. I hoped that she would appreciate my efforts, despite the lack of any clues about her to inform my recipe.

After what seemed like days slaving away in the kitchen (but was, in reality, only six hours) their romantic dinner was ready. I carefully transported my creation to the dining room and, after giving the couple a gentle nudge to wake them, lit the candle in the centre of the table, pulled up a chair and sat down.

Looking back, I might have done a few things differently. For starters, I would have made starters. And perhaps a preliminary visit would have been a good idea in order to familiarise myself with the topography of their kitchen – and microwave. It was a much newer model than mine and the control panel had me baffled for several hours.

But the important thing was that they enjoyed a romantic meal, and sitting there, I could clearly see the love in their eyes. Or it may have been the smoke – I perhaps should have brought a regular candle rather than one of our mosquito-repelling ones but, as I kept telling them, you can't be too careful, what with global warming and so on. Given that I only had the wife's name to go on, I was particularly proud of the main course/dessert (knowing how busy modern couples are, I opted for one of my famous 'two-in-one' specials) and I'm certain they enjoyed tucking into my Selina Moody Stew.

And get them into the mood it certainly did – how could it fail? Oysters, asparagus, ginseng and Viagra, all swimming in my special strawberry and chocolate gravy. Once they had finally finished it all (I always insist on clean plates), the effect was incredible. I had been prepared for a little amorous horse-play but the plate-smashing and yelling was excessive – even by Stephen's standards. Never one to outstay my welcome, I calmly stood up from the table and asked for my payment before departing. The rest is a bit of a blur – largely due to the smoke. Not from the candle, which had long since been extinguished, but from the kitchen. The only thing I remember was being escorted forcibly from the building and being told in no uncertain terms that I would most definitely not be receiving any kind of payment for my services.

I drove home in a despondent state. I just couldn't understand what was wrong. After all, it had been no different from almost every romantic dinner I had cooked for Stephen. However, the following morning I woke to find an envelope on the doormat. Clearly, they had had a change of heart and sent the payment after all. I sighed with relief as I tore it open and removed the contents. But instead of a cheque there was a letter on headed notepaper, demanding financial recompense for, in their words, a ruined evening. Also a ruined tablecloth, dining table, dining room, kitchen and marriage. It was only then that I realised my error – Tom wasn't a barista. He was a barrister.

ROMANTIC GESTURES

As unlikely as it sounds, there are ways to express your affection for your partner that don't involve food or tea. Although, I'm afraid to say that, being a typical man, Stephen hasn't the faintest idea about romantic gestures. On one occasion, he thought it would be a romantic gesture to stand in the garden, singing up at the bedroom window, naked from the waist down apart from a small red flower sticking out of the top of his you-know-what – Poppycock!

POETRY

Being something of a semi-professional poet, the muse often catches me and I find myself putting pen to paper in the name of romance. Nothing says 'I love you' more clearly than an expertly crafted sonnet or haiku. Sometimes short is sweet as is the case with this brief but touching piece I penned to Stephen only recently.

How do I love thee?
Let me count the kids.

I think that says it all. Sadly, Stephen struggles to express his feelings on paper. He did attempt a love poem once but never got further than 'There once was a woman called Edna ...'

PHYSICAL EXPRESSION

Some couples choose to express their love in more physical ways – even in public. They may hold hands or share a tender kiss in the park. While personally I can't say I approve of such displays, I understand that for certain people they can be acceptable.

Of course, different cultures have different social rules. While the British would never countenance such behaviour, it is perfectly common to see an Italian gentleman smacking his girlfriend's bottom as a show of affection. Or his wife's. Or, as was the case on our bargain break to Rome, someone else's wife's. Anywhere else I would have objected in no uncertain terms – that goes without saying. However, as the saying goes, 'when in Rome', so I smacked him back on his bottom. I don't remember the exact sequence of events that followed, but it included the police fishing him out of the Trevi Fountain and cautioning Stephen with aggravated use of a pepper grinder.

SURPRISE GIFTS

Of course, the most romantic gesture is usually some kind of surprise. An unexpected gift can be just the thing to rekindle those romantic embers. Flowers, chocolates etc are all very well but if you really want to surprise your partner, try putting a little more thought into it. The more unusual a gift, the more time they will know you've put into it. Although do be careful – naming a star after your loved one can be terribly romantic. Naming a hurricane, less so.

LOVE LETTERS

I have a shoe box under the bed crammed full of love letters, all tied up with a pink ribbon. Each one is beautifully written, heartfelt and romantic. They're caring, compassionate and deeply moving. They're the most precious things I own. That's why I've never given them to Stephen – he'd never appreciate them. Although, it would be unfair to suggest that Stephen is incapable of writing anything romantic. I keep his one and only love letter with me at all times. I say letter, it's more of a note. Written on a betting slip. But it does say, in bold capitals, '**MY BELOVED**'. He insists that was the name of the horse he was betting on but I know better. Why else would he have written 'Each way' beneath it, if not to emphasise the extent of his love?

Sadly, as your marriage progresses you will find the love letters dry up but don't worry, this is perfectly normal. It doesn't mean that the love has disappeared, merely that that initial intensity has mellowed into something more comfortable. And predictable. Some might even say dull. And just as those early fireworks fade to be replaced by a low energy light bulb, so those flowery letters are replaced by shorter but no less poignant notes such as 'put the bins out' and 'your dinner's in the baby'.

While he rarely puts pen to paper, Stephen has been known to express himself in the written word. For a while, he would secretly write little messages in the steam on the bathroom mirror with his finger for me to discover the next time I had a bath. (Quick tip: If you are thinking of employing this tactic as a romantic surprise, try using phrases such as 'I Love You' and 'Be Mine' rather than 'Red Rum' and 'I know where you live'. While I appreciated the gesture, the exorcist was an expense I could have done without.) And he also wrote me a song. I say wrote, I mean sang. Well, made up when the actual words got stuck on the karaoke machine the other week. Still, it was quite romantic. Quite …

A Staircase To Stephen

There's a lady who makes me Spam fritters of gold,
And she's climbing the staircase to Stephen.
When she gets here I know, if the door isn't closed,
With her brolly, she's going to get even.
Ooh, ooh and she's climbing that staircase to Stephen.

There's three ducks on the wall but she wants to be sure,
'Cause she knows sometimes birds have two meanings.
I just lie here and wait, contemplating my fate
Hoping all of my crimes are forgiven
Ooh, but she makes me wander
Ooh, if only she were blonder

There's a feeling I get when I take off my vest
And I know that my dander's up for it
In the dark she has seen something poke through the sheets
But she stands there and tries to ignore it
Ooh, and it makes me wonder
Ooh, if she were ten years younger

If she blew my bassoon, then we'd both be in tune
And the bedroom would echo with laughter
Then a new day would dawn when we woke on the lawn
And we'd live happily ever after

If there's a woman in the wardrobe, don't be alarmed now,
She's just there looking for her brother
Yes, there are two more on the landing, a misunderstanding
We thought you'd gone to see your mother
What a dreadful blunder

My wife's succumbing and she won't go, as if I don't know
Her Stephen's calling her to join him
Dear Edna, can you shut the window 'cos did you know
Your hairdo flies in the whistling wind?

And as we wander down life's road
Her shadow's shorter than before
There walks a lady very slow
With faded sight and hair like snow
Her hearing aid is running low

But if she listens very hard

That tune will come to her again

As soon as she has had her op, yeah

To have a hip and not to hop

And she'll be riding that stairlift to Stephen ...

PET NAMES

One simple way in which couples express their feelings for each other is the use of pet names. These can have some kind of deep significance, perhaps reflecting a shared experience, or they can just be silly little names which could be quite embarrassing if uttered in public. Fortunately, Stephen and I have no such qualms. But then, why would he object to being called Shnooky-wookykins, Snuggletrousers or Mr Floppy in front of complete strangers? After all, I have no concerns about him calling me Edna. Although I have noticed he tends to reserve the rest of his pet names for when we're in the throes of passion. Kylie and Beyonce are his current favourites.

MISCELLANEOUS

If you wish to make an indelible statement to demonstrate your undying love for your partner, you might consider a tattoo (these can also be used to demonstrate your undying love for your mother, your favourite football team or anchors).

Of course, such an undertaking should not be approached without a degree of caution. Just like marriage, a tattoo is designed to be permanent and can only be rectified with laser surgery (although laser surgery should only be used as a solution to marriage after all other possibilities have been explored). I know only too well the agonies suffered by the wearer of an ill-judged tattoo. Mainly because I've inflicted them. I don't know why Stephen can't just have a little black book like other men.

AN EVENING OUT

What could be more romantic than an unexpected evening out arranged by your partner? The thrill of getting dressed up, the anticipation of the night ahead – it's just the thing to add a spark to the most humdrum of marriages. It could be dinner at a romantic restaurant or a trip to the theatre, or perhaps just a simple trip to the local pub – it doesn't matter. The important thing is to break your usual routine and shake up your partner's expectations. You're saying to your spouse, 'I'm wild, unpredictable and devil-may-care' – not that useless lump who just lies on the sofa night after night without lifting a finger to help you cook, clean or take care of the kids.

I vividly remember the time my Stephen whisked me off without warning to a romantic rooftop dinner, of all things! I'm sure you will have seen those glitzy Hollywood rom-coms where the girl thinks she is being taken to a restaurant, only to find herself on the roof of her New York apartment block, seated at a beautifully decorated table with a bottle of champagne, caviar and an umbrella of stars … this was nothing like that. To be fair to him, Stephen did his best but we were battling against the slope of our terraced house roof from the start. And the frost didn't help. Or the hailstones. Still, it was memorable and at least the new guttering prevented any fatalities.

A WEEKEND AWAY

You've had a hard week – your boss has been impossible, the kids have been unbearable, you're exhausted mentally and physically. Then your spouse comes bursting through the door with a big grin on their face and tells you to pack your bags. Once you've apologised for throwing the baby's nappy at them and they've explained that they've arranged for the children to stay with their parents and booked a nice little B&B in the country for you both, you fling your arms round them and give them a huge kiss. Or a firm handshake, depending how demonstrative you are.

No matter what your work or home life is like, everyone needs a break now and then. Especially if you have children. A weekend away without having to think about the office or domestic chores can be just the ticket. You can recharge your batteries and return ready to take on life all over again. And most importantly you can reacquaint yourself with your partner in a stress-free environment and remind yourself why you married them in the first place. Hopefully.

If you really want to recapture the excitement of being a young as-yet-unmarried couple in love, here are a few tips.

1. Book into the hotel or B&B under an assumed name – Mr and Mrs Smith is a generally accepted pseudonym for an unmarried couple (unless, of course, those are your actual names, in which case use another one). If you are paying by credit card, this will add an extra frisson as the hotel manager calls for the police. Should this be the case, you have two choices – the first is to own up and give your real names, the second I call the Bonnie and Clyde option.

2. Book into the honeymoon suite if there is one in your chosen establishment. If not, book the best room available (preferably a double) and take along a few items to give it that extra romantic atmosphere. While your partner carries the luggage up to the room (the receptionist will be only too happy to place an Out of Order sign on the lift for a small extra fee) run ahead with the key and make a few simple preparations. Place a bottle of champagne (or sparkling wine) in an ice bucket on the table (or fold-down ironing board), lay his and hers matching silk (or silk-effect) robes on the bed and place a chocolate on their pillow. Depending on the kind of weekend you anticipate, this could be an after dinner mint or a family-size Toblerone.

3. Research the local area for suitably romantic places to visit – these could be woodland walks, quiet leafy lanes, secluded meadows or a jousting tournament.

4. When booking a room for a romantic weekend, take into consideration the name of the establishment. You should feel reasonably confident of a place called The Maison

D'Amour or Valentine Cottage – possibly less so of Bates Motel.

The important thing to remember is that no matter how bad you are at cooking or how unromantic you may be (and I should know, dears), never stop trying – your marriage may depend on it! Whether by food, romantic gesture or emergency surgical procedure, there's always a way to a man's (or woman's) heart.

CHAPTER FOUR

An Englishwoman's Home

(NB While I am aware that the more commonly recognised phrase is 'an Englishman's home is his castle', I can assure you that Stephen and I certainly don't live in a castle — even if there is a sign reading 'Camelot' attached to the stone-cladding. Also, I think it is generally accepted that the home is the woman's domain — or at least will be, according to our pre-nup.)

YOUR FIRST HOME TOGETHER

WHEN seeking out your first home together, remember those three magic words — Location, Location, Location. Whatever you do, don't arrange to see a property when that's on. The ideal time is mid-afternoon, allowing you plenty of time between *Jeremy Kyle* and *Deal or No Deal* for a relaxing viewing and a nice cup of tea after.

What kind of place should you be looking for? Inevitably, a young couple just starting out on the property ladder will need to compromise but ideally you should try to find somewhere that reflects both of your personalities. In our case, this was fairly easy as Stephen didn't so much have a personality as a slightly irritating presence. But be careful — one of the biggest nightmares for anyone moving into a new property is finding yourself stuck next to the neighbours from hell. This was unfortunately the case when Stephen and I moved into our first house. I remember it vividly to this day – the all-night parties, the constant slanging matches, the bins of rubbish being emptied over the fence. This went on for months until finally they had enough and moved out.

As it can be a bit of a marital minefield, here's a useful A to Z list covering all aspects of the home, as I feel these things should never be approached blindly or unalphabetically.

AN A TO Z OF THE HOME

A

Attic – The attic is a wonderfully useful space, sitting unobtrusively at the top of your house like an undiscovered serial killer. You may choose to use this space by converting it into an extra bedroom, office or sex chamber – just don't forget to get the appropriate planning permission, or in the last case, inappropriate planning permission.

Personally, I prefer to use our attic as a storage space. Out of sight, out of mind, as the saying goes and it's the perfect spot for those little best-forgotten knick-knacks such as my wedding dress, the wedding photographs and the children. I also insist Stephen keeps his Scalextric up there, together with his life-size portrait which I have to admit I find a little disturbing – while Stephen has decayed terribly over the years, it hasn't aged a single day.

B

Bathroom Etiquette – Rubber ducks are acceptable. Real ducks are not. Nor are geese, swans, moorhens or crested grebes. If in doubt, avoid wildfowl reserves on bath days.

A husband and wife sharing a bath is perfectly acceptable provided it is for the express purpose of saving water provided of course that the husband sits at the tap end. Alternatively, half a dozen bricks provide the same benefit as well as being more entertaining company.

One of the most common causes of marital discord is the perennial leaving-up-of-the-toilet-seat issue. Fortunately, this isn't the case in the Fry house as Stephen so rarely makes it as far as the bathroom.

Beams – Nothing gives a room more delightful mock Tudor pub character than beams. Preferably oak, although other woods are acceptable – the important thing is that they are sturdy, especially if, like me, you have a particularly tall husband. They carry the additional charm of affording me the regular sight of him banging his head.

Bed – The most important item of furniture in the bedroom is, of course, the bed, hence the name. Buying the marital bed can be a tricky task. It can be difficult to work out which kind to get unless you know long your marriage will last. Some couples may require a bed strong enough to last for many decades whereas for others, a camp bed is perfectly adequate. If we take 25 years as the average marriage length (don't worry, dears, it's nothing like as long as that), then you will need to choose a sturdy wooden structure designed for the job. Similarly, you should choose a mattress to match your marriage – for example, for the first few years it should be firm but springy. After five years it should still have a bit of bounce. 10 years on, it should be comfortable and forgiving although there may be the occasional unexpected poke (easily solved by a trip to the manufacturer, assuming it's still under warranty), and after 25 years, it should be saggy, lifeless and ready for the scrap heap.

The Bedroom Mirror is also a highly important item. It needn't be especially ornate but should be full-length to allow you and your partner to see what they look like from top to toe. Of course, couples of a certain age such as Stephen and, to an extent, myself may prefer a more forgiving and less revealing length. For those couples, I would recommend a mirror no greater than 60 centimetres in length, which also has the advantages of being quicker to clean and easier to affix to the ceiling above the bed.

Bedroom Storage – The division of storage in the bedroom is one which should be addressed as soon as possible. Space can be at a premium, assuming you don't have a walk-in wardrobe (which can pose its own problems – in Stephen's case, nightmares about lions and witches). It's very important that both husband and wife have sufficient space for their needs. I need room for my hats and Stephen needs room for when he comes in from one of his pub crawls and can't find the bathroom – or, as he calls it, a wardrobe malfunction.

C

Ceilings – Often overlooked, or underlooked I should say, the humble ceiling plays a surprisingly big role in the impression of space in a room. Without one, you get a really accurate impression of space, particularly at night.

Cellar – Whether for wine, lager or expired vagrants, a good cellar is a welcome addition to any home.

Chimney Breast – I really don't have anything to say about this. Stephen insisted I include it because he likes the word 'breast'. And chimney, strangely.

Class – The way you choose to decorate your home says everything about you. From the quality of jokes on your toilet rolls to the trajectory of your flying ducks to the type of plastic fruit in your bowl (bananas or kumquats), your entire house is a testament to your class, or lack of it. However, if you lack any discernable sense of taste, don't panic. Here are just a few handy hints to help you present your home in the best possible light.

1. Present your home in the best possible light. Change those dead bulbs and give that Elvis lamp a jolly good dusting.

2. Don't worry about that motorbike in the living room – the upper classes are famously idiosyncratic. Simply make a feature of it by draping a stuffed mongoose over the seat and painting the mudguards pink.

3. A log effect fire is a real giveaway. Those mock flames won't provide you with any warmth when you find yourself in the bleak, cold social wilderness. Replace it with a patio heater immediately.

4. First impressions count and being forced to stand on your doorstep listening to the *Birdy Song* will impress no-one. When it comes to doorbells, a simple ding dong is more than adequate. It alerts you to your guest's presence while simultaneously reminding them of Leslie Phillips – far classier.

Conservatory – Essentially a greenhouse for people, a conservatory should be clean, spacious and filled with bags of compost. In the summer, it can make an ideal breakfast room before the daily temperature makes the heat unbearable. Then it makes a perfect granny flat.

Curtains – If, as someone famously once said, your windows are the eyes to your soul (thank you, Vaguelytruepedia.com), that must make your curtains the eyelids (with those fringey bits, the eyelashes and the adjoining damp patch, the mascara). More than mere window-dressing, your curtains can add a touch of flair to your room as well as providing something to position yourself behind when keeping a well-meaning eye on your neighbours. Any number of shades and patterns are available for those wishing to add a colourful accent to a room. And what more colourful accent is there than Welsh, with its delightfuly melodic overtones and endearingly phlegmy aftertaste? A dragon or leek-based design can't fail to attract the attention of your visitors and let's not forget they do *Doctor Who* now too!

D

Doors – Often ignored, your doors can make all the difference between a welcoming family home and an assortment of sealed rooms. Doors come in all shapes and sizes, from ornate oak ones to cat-flaps. But which kind of doors are best for your house? Without wishing to be too prescriptive, I think you'll find the following a useful guide – for the living room I would recommend a living room door, for the kitchen, a kitchen door, for the bedrooms, bedroom doors and for the front of your house, a front door. Additionally, if your house has a back, you might want to consider a back door. This can be particularly useful if, like me, you have regular visits from tradesmen or an especially embarrassing husband, although in my experience it's best not to allow him to get too fond of using your back door (nor the tradesmen, come to that).

E

En-suite – Often found in hotels, en-suite refers to a bedroom with an additional room attached, usually a bathroom rather than a billiard room or a kitchen. While not inexpensive, an en-suite can be an absolute godsend if you or your partner is in the habit of making numerous nightly visits, especially after a night in the Dog & Duck. Stephen certainly makes good use of ours (see Walk-in Wardrobe).

Extensions – Almost inevitably, a couple will reach a point where their house is no longer big enough. This could be due to excessive acquisition of household items, pets or simple contraceptive failure. When this happens, you have two choices. While moving to a larger house can seem the obvious option, it's not without its drawbacks – moving house has been described as the third most irritating thing you can do after dying and getting married. Also, you may have built a strong emotional attachment to your current property and not wish to leave. If this is the case, then an extension could be for you. As with an attic conversion, it's vital to obtain planning permission – we learned this the hard way after Stephen extended our living room into next door's kitchen – but it can be an immensely satisfying experience. There is something almost primeval about man's desire to build and woman's desire to watch him in his string vest. Hmmm ......
now, where was I? Oh yes ... F.

F

Feng Shui – This is the ancient Chinese art of furniture moving. While some sceptics refuse to accept that the position of your furniture can affect your health and fortune, I am a whole-hearted advocate of the system. My ability to enjoy a good night's sleep improved instantly by simply moving our washing machine from the bedroom into the kitchen. And when I moved the sofa from the living room into the back yard, I felt an enormous sense of calm and well-being – despite it being awfully hard to shift with Stephen lying on it.

Fireplace – generally the best place for a fire. Why tamper with tradition? Or the fire, as I've said to Stephen on numerous occasions – usually in a speeding ambulance.

Fish bowl – This can be useful in a number of ways – as well as providing a habitat for fish, it can provide a nice water feature for your hallway and a receptacle for car keys on more adventurous social occasions.

Flow – Interior decorators are always talking about the flow of a house. This is achieved by seamless design which leads the eye and the beholder effortlessly from one room to another. This is a great deal harder than it sounds, especially when you and your partner have such divergent tastes as me and mine. The nearest we get to a sense of flow is when Stephen falls asleep in the bath with the taps running – then it's possible for me to mop seamlessly throughout the entire house.

Focal point – A focal point is usually some form of static object which draws the eye and provides a topic of conversation for visitors. This could be an unusual clock, a striking figurine or, in my case, Stephen (this may seem a little harsh but as Stephen himself says when I ask him to move – there's focal point. At least, that's what I think he says).

Fridge – The fridge is the heart of any home, the family fuel tank. However, it needn't be a purely functional item. A fridge can also make a statement – or several, if you have enough magnetic letters. Buying the right one can be a daunting experience. Generally, the ruder-sounding the name, the better the fridge. Smegs are very highly rated, as are Wenkas and Cunds (N B this also applies to bedroom furniture, where you simply can't beat Fugkin bedsteads).

Furniture – Whether you sit on it, sleep on it or eat your dinner off it (or all three at once, in Stephen's case), there's no ignoring the importance of furniture in the family home. As a rule, the more you pay for your furniture, the longer it will last.

G

Garden – Traditionally, the garden was the man's domain. He would till the soil, mow the grass and tend the vegetables. When we moved into our first house, Stephen was terribly enthusiastic, keen to recreate the seventies BBC sitcom, *The Good Life*. His interest soon waned, however, when it became clear cauliflowers wouldn't grow on a concrete yard and you couldn't get Felicity Kendal from the local garden centre. The truth is, I'm not sure what Stephen wants but I'm pretty sure he needs decking.

Something else you may wish to have in your garden is what experts call a water feature. It's important to opt for something proportionate in size and tone to the rest of your garden such as a lily pond or small fountain not, as Stephen insisted on, a 1:1 scale recreation of the Universal Studios tour in Florida. It's patently inappropriate for a small suburban terrace, although I have to admit it can be fun watching the reactions of passers-by as they're drenched by the 20-foot animatronic shark.

H

Housework – One of the major causes of marital disharmony is the division of labour in the home. If you don't establish the ground rules early on, you are setting yourselves up for years of drudgery and resentment. Like most modern women, I have no desire to be chained to the kitchen sink – unless it's purely recreational. Like Stephen, however, many husbands are still resistant to doing their share around the house, seeing putting out the bins and opening jars as the limit of their domestic responsibility. On the odd occasion I actually managed to persuade Stephen to do the washing-up, he would deliberately perform the task as inadequately as possible, although I didn't fall for that in the kitchen any more than in the bedroom. Eventually, my only recourse was to outwit him – something that would require at least 10 per cent of my guile.

Like so many men, Stephen is a competitive animal and so I introduced an element of sporting endeavour to the daily household chores. Now, he's only too happy to represent his country in Extreme Washing-up, Australian Rules Hoovering, Pro-celebrity Toilet Cleaning and Synchronised Scrubbing. It may cost me a small fortune in prize money, medals and sponsorship deals but it's worth it.

I

Island – Not literally an island, of course, but a free standing kitchen unit. Often topped with granite or some other equally ostentatious material, it doubles as a food preparation area and somewhere to lean when you're having one of your turns.

J

Jurassic Park – Just one of the many wallpaper designs I refuse to let Stephen choose.

K

Kitchen – You may call me old-fashioned but I still regard the kitchen as strictly the woman's domain. Many argue, pointing out that the majority of top chefs are male and while I accept that I could never hope to compete with their colourful turns of phrase, I maintain that when it comes to good, traditional, edible cuisine what you really need is a woman. And a can opener. And a microwave.

L

Lighting – It's possible to alter the whole personality of a room by your choice of lighting. A fluorescent strip will give it a stark, clinical look whereas strategically placed uplighters will create a more relaxed mood. If the bulb in your bedroom is too bright it can be detrimental to you-know-what. I asked Stephen to change ours but he wasn't able to which is a little depressing, although to be fair to him he has just recently got a little dimmer.

Lounge or **Living Room** – It's up to you. Personally, I prefer lounge.

M

Maintenance – Household maintenance, or DIY as it has become known, is traditionally a male domain but nowadays more and more women are picking up the tool box themselves. In my own case, I often grow tired of waiting for Stephen to put up a shelf or fix a cupboard door and find myself forced to pick up a hammer myself. After no more than half a dozen carefully administered blows, he's generally more than willing to carry out the required task. Of course, when it comes to more expert jobs such as plumbing or changing a light bulb, I always insist on calling a professional. Not only do they provide an efficient service, they are usually willing, for a small additional fee, to satisfy my womanly needs – such as shifting Stephen off the sofa so I can watch *Emmerdale*.

Mirrors – There's more to mirrors than meets the eye, as Alice discovered. As well as enabling you to check your appearance (with or without your husband writhing above you), they can also create the illusion of greater space in a room. A relatively small room can appear almost double the size by the simple addition of a couple of large mirrors. (WARNING – be careful not to position your mirrors on opposite walls as this creates a portal to an infinite number of universes and before you know it you'll be sucked into some kind of vortex and miss *Diagnosis Murder*.)

Additionally, a mirror can be an invaluable aid in food preparation. By simply holding one under Stephen's nose, I can confidently predict the amount of food I need to prepare.

N

Nest of Tables – An odd phrase, this – almost suggesting that tables are hatched from eggs laid by giant birds and we all know that's ridiculous. In fact, I'll just check Vaguelytruepedia.com to check the real derivation of the term ...

O

Oh – Apparently they are.

Ottoman – Not, as Stephen thought, a Spider-Man villain, but a padded footstool.

Oven – If the fridge is the family fuel tank, the oven is its engine, taking in the fuel, or food, and heating it up to, er, make the steering wheel go ... I'm terribly sorry, dears – I really don't know anything about cars.

P

Pantry – Not a place to keep your pants, as the name suggests, but a small storage room for your cooking items, ingredients and utensils. And Stephen's pants.

Photos, **Pictures** and **Prints** – If you want to liven up a drab wall, the easiest way to do so is to hang up a picture. It could be a nice photograph of something personal – or your family – or possibly, an attractive print.

Poker-Playing Dogs – See *Photos, Pictures and Prints*. And *Class*.

Q

Quirky – When something deviates from the norm, it's known as quirky. Or kinky. Either way, I'm having none of it in my house.

R

Retro – A highly popular theme for many houses – and relatively inexpensive too, provided you're prepared to wait long enough.

S

Scandinavia – I'm sure you can't have failed to notice the ever-increasing influence of Scandinavia in our homes. I'm proud to say that our household is completely up-to-date with this. Thanks to Stephen Junior and Viennetta, the house is a continual procession of girls in ill-fitting jumpers with dragon tattoos and incomprehensible would-be murderers.

Shower – Popularised by the famous Alfred Hitchcock documentary on motel bathrooms, the shower has become as fundamental an aspect of the bathroom as the bath itself. It is also quicker to use and saves water, second in both only to Stephen's favourite – not bothering to get washed at all.

Sofas – The most important item of furniture in your living room, you should take your time choosing exactly the right one for your needs. A good sofa should be able to withstand the weight of one adult male for up to 16 hours per day and have ample space behind the cushions for approximately 10 pounds in loose change, half a dozen items of underwear, several TV guides and the odd baby.

Skirting Boards – Not to be underestimated, the apparently insignificant skirting board is an essential component of any room. Without it there would be a sizeable gap between the wall and the floor and consequently the most terrible draughts.

Sinks – Have you heard of the phrase, 'Everything but the kitchen sink'? Well, you'll be pleased to know it doesn't apply to this chapter, dears! How could it? Without the kitchen sink, one can only imagine the state of the average family kitchen. Plus, there would be one reason fewer to wear rubber gloves (see bedroom).

Spare Room – If you are fortunate enough to find yourselves with a spare room in your new home, you may face a difficult decision – how best should you use it? Stephen and I found ourselves in this position when we bought our first property and it took several weeks to resolve the issue. I wanted to use it as a guest room for friends and family to use when they visited and Stephen wanted it to store his back issues of *Razzle* magazine. Finally we managed to reach a compromise – we used it as a bedroom for the children, which then freed up the garden shed for Stephen's magazines.

T

Tea Room – Obviously, no home would be complete without such a room. Where else would you keep your dozens of teapots and scores of kettles? Where else would you put your many caddies and your teaspoon collection? Where else could you spend the afternoon relaxing to the sound of that bubbling water and the scent of PG tips? Fortunately, our house has the perfect Tea Room – well, it is now I've moved the twins' beds out.

Technology – If you're as fond of gadgets as my Stephen (I often can't move for the piles of DVD players and mobile phones he has stacked up throughout the house – although, to be fair to him, they generally disappear as quickly as they arrive – often in virtual silence in the middle of the night) your idea of the dream home would be some kind of high-tech apartment. But before you head blindly into this futuristic fantasy world, a note of caution, dears. While these seemingly utopian dwellings might be very appealing, there is a darker side as anyone who has saw the 1977 documentary *Demon Seed* will attest. While I fully appreciate the attraction of such amenities as electric doors and remote-controlled curtains, I draw the line at impregnation by a malevolent computer. It's quite bad enough with Stephen, thank you very much.

Themes – When deciding how to decorate your house, it's important to decide on a theme. Stephen and I spent several long weeks discussing this when we first moved into our current home but struggled to reach common ground. I favoured a rustic theme with a farmhouse kitchen and natural textures throughout the house whereas he preferred the theme from *Shaft*. In the end, we arrived at a compromise – I ignored him and he went to the pub.

U

Underfloor Heating – An extremely desirable feature of any home.

Underfloor Indian Burial Ground – A less desirable feature of any home (see also – *television repairs*)

V

Veranda – Found at the back of the house, a raised platform from which to view the garden.

Veronica – Also found at the back of the house. And under the bed. And in the airing cupboard. Stephen's not fooling anyone when he says she likes to play hide and seek.

W

Walk-in Wardrobe – This is usually a feature of more interest to the wife, although when we were looking for our first marital home (in this instance the word 'first' applies here to 'home' not 'marital' although I still live in hope), the one thing Stephen insisted on was a walk-in wardrobe. The novelty soon wore off, however, when he discovered it wasn't quite as large as he had envisaged, nor did it contain any talking lions. For me, it was no more enticing – unlike many women, I've never seen the need for countless dresses or pairs of shoes. As far as I'm concerned, as long as they're made of good, sturdy leather and can withstand rain and dog mess that's all you need. And the same applies to shoes.

Wet Room – Supposedly a relatively new development, a wet room is essentially an entire room filled with water, although I have to say that Stephen created the concept several years ago – and every year since, on the occasion of his annual bath.

Wicker – Whether it's a chair, a laundry basket or a giant pagan sacrificial figure, you can't do better than wicker – light, fashionable and equally uncomfortable no matter which of the aforementioned uses to which you put it.

Windows – They can be single-, double- or even triple-glazed but all windows serves the same purpose – to enable you to sit all day staring hopelessly out at the grey, empty world, wondering how you came to be stuck here with six or seven children and a husband whose idea of a cultural evening is a seat at Monster Trucks on Ice and whose idea of romance is two seats at Monster Trucks on Ice.

X

Xylophones, **X-ray Machines**, **X-Men Origins: Wolverine** – to be perfectly honest with you, dears, this is little more than a list of words beginning with X. If I were you, I'd move on to Y ...

Y

Yak, **Yemen**, **Yoko Ono** ... well, maybe on to Z, then ...

Z

Zebra – Got you, dears! Contrary to what you may have been thinking, this isn't merely a randomly chosen word beginning with Z. Zebra stripes make a bold fashion statement in your home, whether on your cushions, your bedspread or even your kitchen units (if you're looking to make an even bolder statement, use the whole zebra).

CHAPTER FIVE

Between The Sheets

As a married couple, there is one subject it's very important to discuss openly and frankly, and that's the subject of 'you-know-what'.

Without you-know-what, you and I wouldn't exist – it's fundamental to life and, so I'm led to believe, pleasure. You-know-what is everywhere – on billboards, on television, on the sides of buses. There are you-know-what magazines, you-know-what shops on the high street, even you-know-what-on-the-beach cocktails. As the advertising industry so succinctly puts it, 'You-know-what sells.'

And yet it's still important, in this age of permissiveness and *Hollyoaks*, to remember the real purpose of you-know-what. No, dears, not procreation – that's merely an unfortunate side-effect. The real purpose is to annoy your neighbours. Without that, it's meaningless. Why else would a couple bounce up and down, grunting and howling like a pair of rabid baboons (or in our case, one rabid baboon and his reluctant handler)?

POSITIONS

There are, apparently, several different positions in which to engage in you-know-what. One of Stephen's favourites is called, I think, the Below Job – presumably because the wife is positioned somewhat lower than her spouse. I won't go into too many details aside from saying it's a little tough on the knees and if it's not quite to your taste, it's probably best just to take it on the chin. His other favourite is the wheelbarrow, which involves me wheeling him home from the pub in a barrow.

Of course, Stephen is rather more outspoken than me on this subject – indeed, he's a veritable carnal thesaurus. Here are his current 50 favourite words to describe you-know-what – and believe me, dears, these are only the tip of the iceberg...

STEVEN'S 50 WORDS FOR YOU-KNOW-WHAT

(With my deepest apologies to you all, particularly the lovely Kate Bush. Don't worry, dear – the ankle bracelet's been firmly re-attached.)

1. Boinking
2. Doinking
3. Barry White-out

4. The Eagle Has Landed
5. Crumpet
6. Geese-a-laying
7. Vesuvius
8. Peperami Party
9. Mount Edna
10. Rumpy-pumpy
11. Making the Beast with Two Backsides
12. Parking the Purple Porsche
13. Humpalumpa
14. Taking little Stephen to the Toy Shop
15. Straddlesplashing
16. Nookie
17. Up Periscope!
18. Widdecombe Wept
19. Googling
20. Up-a-down Penguins
21. Torso Trembler
22. Doing the Fandango
23. Nomisterfloppy
24. Towering Inferno
25. Boiler-bunnying
26. Packing the Trunk
27. Whisky-frisky
28. Kebabarama
29. Boingy Boingy
30. Sodastreaming
31. Slappaccino

32. Going for Gold
33. How's Your Father
34. How's Your Mother
35. Where's Your Sister
36. Thrustathon
37. Letting Loose the Light Saber
38. Scaramangabanga
39. Hammer Time
40. The Vanishing Vuvuzela
41. Crème Passionnelle
42. Flobadobadob
43. Where's Willy
44. Bad for Backs
45. Fumblecustard
46. Didgeridooing It
47. Jiggery Pokery
48. Anointing the Archbishop
49. Dipping the Dongle
50. Frying Tonight!

FANTASIES

It's not uncommon for husbands and wives to secretly fanta-sise about someone else during you-know-what. However, some people are better at keeping these fantasies secret than others. Personally, I would never reveal any of my imaginary paramours whereas Stephen is rather less discreet, often shouting out a name from his extensive celebrity fantasy list at the peak of his excitement. On occasion he recites the entire list which, while mildly distracting, does have the detrimental effect of extending the process beyond the usual three minutes.

Some couples even take this process one step further by actually putting pen to paper and compiling lists of celebrities they are 'allowed to sleep with' should the opportunity arise. I wouldn't normally condone such permissiveness but when he heard about this, Stephen insisted we each write down – and publish – our own list. And so, with a degree of reluctance, here they are.

My List

1 Sir Elton John (if only he weren't already married)
2 Sir Ian McKellen (a true gentleman with a child-like twinkle)
3 Graham Norton (cheeky, red-blooded Irish charmer)
4 John Barrowman (the traditional lantern-jawed ladies' man)
5 Hugh Laurie (can't think how he got on the list. In fact, I've never heard of him and neither have any of my children – especially Hugh Junior.)

Stephen's List

1 Beyonce (apparently she's bootylicious, whatever that is)
2 Pan's People (who count as one, apparently, due to their perfectly synchronised movements)
3 Jessica Rabbit (he assures me she's not an actual rabbit)
4 The woman at the post office (not technically a celebrity although surprisingly well-known)
5 Pretty much anyone who's up for it

Of course, it's important not to take these lists too seriously. They should be regarded as whimsical flights of fancy and not, as in Stephen's case, a legally-enforceable set of instructions.

FOREPLAY

The key to foreplay is not to rush it. It should be a slow, tantalising process. I would suggest a gentle back rub with essential oils – or if your budget is limited, a few non-essential ones. Tell your spouse to lie down on their front. A professional masseuse would have a special table with a hole for the client to put his or her face through but if a massage table is beyond your means, I find setting up a camp bed next to the toilet equally effective (and has a useful secondary function should your partner have over-indulged). If you and your partner are particularly close, you could ask them to roll up or even remove their top beforehand. To avoid shocking your partner, I would recommend warming the oil in your hands before letting it touch their skin – rather than in the deep fat fryer (not a mistake I'll make again – our chips tasted terrible for weeks).

Once the oil has reached body temperature, apply it carefully to the back, making sure it doesn't seep over the sides onto the bed sheets or kitchen table. Then, using your palms, rub the oil gently into the skin using a slow, circular motion. Gradually increase the pressure until you can feel the muscles in your partner's back become more pliant, like pizza base mix (resist the temptation to add tomato puree and mozzarella at this point – there's plenty of time for that later).

And that's really all there is to it. If you've followed the steps correctly, your partner should be feeling completely relaxed. You may choose to extend the process to include legs, arms and other less attractive areas but hopefully, they'll be asleep by now. If not, make them a nice mug of Ovaltine and you should be able to get on with reading your book in peace.

FAKING IT

If your foreplay technique isn't up to scratch or, like my Stephen, your partner's simply a bit of an animal, you still have one more option – fake it. It doesn't matter what it is – headache, toothache, your own death – just so long as you don't actually have to do 'it'. This way, you will guarantee a long and happy physical relationship and it doesn't need to involve you. As that dreadful creature on the insurance adverts says – Easy!

DRESSING TO IMPRESS

If, in spite of the previous paragraphs, you still want to get your partner in the mood, you can try wearing provocative lingerie – perhaps something black and lacy. Women can try this too, although personally, I prefer to wear something a touch more discreet. I find that it adds to the mystery and enflames Stephen's ardour far more than anything too revealing. I have an entire range of more sophisticated items guaranteed to knock his socks off, unless he's removed them himself for once.

Firstly, there's my baby doll nightie – a racy, full-length flannelette number with an iron-on picture of Tiny Tears on the front. Then there's my see-through nightcap (actually it's a Travelodge shower-cap, which you're perfectly entitled to take if you're a guest, along with those small bottles of shampoo, the towels and the television – according to Stephen). But my piece de resistance, the things that really drive my husband wild, are my crochetless panties (I knitted them instead). All of which play their part in keeping Stephen's ardour on a steady flame (rather than boiling over). He even refers to me as his 'Mother I Like to Do Everything With' – or MILDEW. He's so sweet.

For his part, Stephen is often only too happy to parade around in his Phantom Menace pyjamas for my pleasure (or so he chooses to believe). Sometimes he even performs a strip-tease, slowly and carefully removing one item of clothing after another before triumphantly flinging his Y-fronts in the air while gyrating balletically to whatever music the shopping centre happens to be playing at the time.

ROLE-PLAY

Some couples like to add a little spice to their nocturnal activities by pretending to be someone else. Stephen's constantly asking me to dress up as Princess Leia from *Star Wars* but the hairdo really doesn't work with my hat so he invariably has to settle for a Han Solo. I have to admit I did once agree to par-

ticipate in his plumber/bored housewife role-play fantasy – I
waited in all day and he never turned up.

KEEPING THE MAGIC ALIVE

One question I often hear from my married friends is 'Does
he still fancy me?'. I tell them straight, 'Of course he does,
Stephen fancies anything in a skirt – or tracksuit bottoms.'
Then they say to me, 'Well, obviously, but what about my
husband? Does he still find me attractive after all these years?'
to which my reply is always the same – 'Of course not, dear
– don't be ridiculous.'

The plain and simple truth is that, apart from a very select
group including Madonna, Tina Turner and myself, women
invariably lose their allure as they grow older. In desperation,
some turn to cosmetic surgery but this can be risky – as I
always say, a moment on the hips, a lifetime on the lips. If
you're determined to remain attractive to your partner,
instead of this drastic course of action I would recommend
you simply adopt a healthy diet and exercise regime. Below
are a few of the plans I have created, especially with the
slightly more middle-aged woman in mind.

The 70s Plan
Not designed for septuagenarians (well, not exclusively, any-
way), this plan takes as its inspiration the golden age of flares
and mirror balls, the 1970s.
Typical daily food intake – Skinless Chicken in a Basket, Prawn
Cocktail (in a small glass), Black Forest Gateau – one thin

slice, half a packet of Spangles, one glass of Diet Blue Nun.
Exercises – the Space-hopper, the Hustle and the Funky Gibbon.

The Yo-yo Diet

Typical daily food intake – anything you like, provided the amount varies wildly from day to day.
Exercises – Walk the dog, loop the loop and that one where it seems to stop at the bottom of the string before it comes up again really fast.

In addition, for the rhythmically-inclined, I have developed my own range of physically demanding Latin American-inspired dance classes – Spamba, Rhumbaba, Lampasanda and, especially for the elderly, my hugely successful Zomba classes.

One of the hardest things about exercising is beating the boredom. Going to the gym can quickly become routine and the exercises repetitive as well as being embarrassing for those quite rightly struggling with their body image. Luckily, last year Stephen and I bought the kids a Nintendo Puu (the games console you play sitting down) which is ideal for those wanting to shed a few pounds in the privacy of their own home. You can buy a variety of stimulating, calorie-burning games, including one designed especially for the beginner – Strenuous Puu, one for the intermediate exerciser – Really Strenuous Puu and one for the advanced – I Wouldn't Go In There For A While, If I Were Yuu.

FETISHES

What is a fetish? I'm perfectly sure I have no idea, dear — you'd better ask Stephen. Whatever they are, they seem to involve a lot of rubber and marmalade. If, however, you're not planning a visit to any of our local hostelries or bookmakers in the foreseeable future, here's a little song I remember hearing on my wireless many years ago that might enlighten you …

> Birds do it, blokes do it,
> Even educated folks do it,
> Let's do it,
> Let's you-know-what.

> Masochists in their masks do it,
> Stalkers with their little tartan flasks do it
> Let's do it,
> Let's you-know-what.

> The mile-high club on long flights do it
> It's every passenger's dream
> Doggers flash their lights to do it
> It's just a car-sharing scheme.

> Exhibitionists on a stand do it,
> Swingers with the Benny Goodman band do it,
> Let's do it,
> Let's you-know-what.

Naturists in the sun do it,
Bondage freaks are not allowed to undo it,
Let's do it,
Let's you-know-what

Transvestites while in their frocks do it,
Necrophiliacs inside a box do it,
Let's do it,
Let's you-know-what

Suburban types behind doors do it,
With a bowlful of keys,
Foot fetishists do it,
They're in it up to their knees

OAPs with a pill do it
Even those with memory failure still do it
Let's do it,
Let's ... er ... ?

CHAPTER SIX

The Clatter of Tiny Feet

E VENTUALLY, no matter how hard you try to avoid them, most marriages are 'blessed' with little ones – tiny bundles of 'joy' that will turn your lives upside down (assuming they were the right way up to begin with). Before you know it, you will have completely forgotten what it's like to have a proper night's sleep, a peaceful car journey and crayon-free walls. Fortunately, being married to Stephen, I was already well used to all of these things.

Our own six or seven children cover quite an age range, a situation arising from Stephen's regular enforced absences spent at his landlord's pleasure. Our first, Stephen Junior, was an accident, or so we tell him. Viennetta came soon afterwards, followed by Hugh Junior (who really was an accident). Brangelina was born a few years later, then there was a bit of a gap before the twins, Asbo an Subo (for a while I thought I had finally discovered a reliable . rm of birth control, namely changing the locks when Stephen went to the pub) and finally, our most recent addition, the baby (we haven't chosen a name yet – we want to see how his or her personality develops before deciding).

So, what advice can I give you for when the stork comes to

visit? Well, firstly, the stork *doesn't* come to visit. I know. It was quite a shock to me too. If anything it was more of a humming bird (although Stephen prefers to call it his albatross of love). But don't worry – childbirth really isn't all that painful. Not compared with the subsequent 18 years. And nowadays, there are all kinds of special drugs designed to numb the whole experience – also terribly effective during conception, I find.

These days, many husbands choose to be at the birth in order to support their wives and be part of this natural miracle, but it isn't compulsory. Personally, I wouldn't recommend it – I found that Stephen just got in the way, constantly mopping my brow, asking if I was alright and playing with the speculum. If, however, your husband insists on being present, I would suggest a little wifely subterfuge (you men don't need to read the following few lines – why not pop down the pub instead, there's a good chap?). When you feel your first contractions, send your man to the supermarket for a pint of milk – or preferably a mini-break to Prague. This should allow you sufficient time to bring his offspring into the world in relative peace. Or better still, don't tell him you're pregnant in the first place. Most modern men are far too polite and/or fearful to mention their wives have put on a few pounds and just imagine the look on his face when he returns home with the groceries or duty-free bottle of Kalhua and 800 Silk Cut to find a beautiful, bouncing, screaming baby in his home! It almost makes the whole unpleasant process worthwhile.

So, now you've got your first child, what do you do with it? Well, dears, the answer is not a lot – apart from feeding it, burping it, changing its nappies and trying to get it to sleep (again, my experience with Stephen meant this was second nature to me). The truth is, once you've got over that initial rush of joy (this can last between a few weeks and a few minutes, depending on your disposition), most babies are actually rather dull. You can't have a decent conversation with them, you can't play chess with them, you can't take them to casinos – all they do is lie there crying. Still, it's important that you treasure this time, as it's the best it's going to get.

Research suggests that a newborn child's three favourite sounds are its mother's voice, its mother's heartbeat and its father's voice – this is because these are the sounds it has been listening to in the womb. Although, curiously, Stephen Junior's three favourite sounds as a baby were a can of lager being opened, the *A-Team* theme tune and the quiz machine at the Dog & Duck.

One question a mother – and to a certain extent, a father – wants to know the answer to when they look at their baby is 'what will he or she be like when they're older?'. It's surprisingly easy to answer this – simply establish the sex of your child. If it's male, it will more than likely grow up to be a boy. If it's female, a girl. I'm sure we'll get around to this eventually – once we've got through all those DVD box sets we got for Christmas.

If, however, you want to know a little more – perhaps his or her personality, looks and even career, you can use astrology. While some people claim it's mumbo jumbo, I firmly believe it has a strong scientific basis and that the moment you are born shapes your whole destiny, as I believe the following research findings conclusively prove –

Monday's child is fair enough,
Tuesday's child is pretty rough,
Wednesday's child is full of woe,
Thursday's child is kind of slow,
Friday's child works hard for a pittance,
Saturday's child likes torturing kittens,
And the child that's born on the Sabbath day is
bonny and blithe, ginger, fond of Michael Buble,
prone to chest infections, plagued with self-doubt,
employed in I.T., unable to pat his head and rub
his stomach at the same time and gay.

If that doesn't convince you, dears, nothing will!

BABY NAMES

Choosing a name for your child can be one of the most important decisions you will make as a couple. It can shape their
personality, their career, even their gender. To help you and
your partner with this potentially life-shaping choice, I have
included an alphabetical list Stephen and I drew up before
naming most of our children (I'm sure you'll be able to work
out which ones are Stephen's).

M = Male, F = Female, M/F = Male or Female

A – Anaglypta (*F*), Anakin (*M*), Anon (*M/F*), Aslan (*M*)

B – Bazza (*M*), Beelzebub (*M*), Beelzebubbles (*F*),

Beowulf (*M*), Bilbo (*M*), Boba (*M*)

C – Chav (*M/F*), Chumbawumba (*F*), Cialis (*F*)

D – Dazza (*M*), Dappy (*M*), Darth (*M*), Dopey (*M*)

E – Edna (*F*), Ella-Ella-Ella (*F*), Elvis (*M*)

F – Fender (*M*), Ferrero (*M*)

G – Gazza (*M*), George-at-asda (*M*), Google (*M/F*),
Gromit (*M*)

H – Hadron (*M*), Han (*M*), Haribo (*M*), Hoodie (*M/F*)

I – Ibiza (*F*), Ike (*M*), Ikea (*F*), Innit (*M*), Innita (*F*)

J – Jabba (*M*), Jar-jar (*M*), Jedward (*M*), Jenga (*F*),
Jojoba (*F*)

K – Kajagoogoo (*M*), Kebab (*M*), Kebabs (*F*), Kerplunk (*M*),
Korma (*F*), Kylie (*F*)

L – Lambrini (*F*), Leia (*F*), Lenor (*M*), Lenora (*F*) Lidl (*M*),
Limahl (*M*), Lol (*M*), Luke (*F*)

M – Masala (*F*), Mega (*M*), Megan (*F*)

N – N'Dubz (*M*), N'Dubya (*F*) Neo (*M*), Nutella (*F*)

O – Omg (*M*)

P – Persil (*M*), Primark (*M*), Primula (*F*)

Q – Qui-Gon (*M*), Qwerty (*M*), Qwerta (*F*)

R – Reebok (*M*), Rocky, Rocky 2, Rocky 3, Rocky 4, Rocky 5 (all *M*) Rofl (*M*)

S – Sambucca (*F*), Shaft (*M*), Shazza (*F*), Skeletor (*M*), Skye (*F*), Skye Plus (*F*), Samantha (*F*), Spartacus (*M*), Spongebob (*M*), Stan (*M*), Stannah (*F*), Stella (*F*), Supermario (*M*), Susudio (?)

T – T K Maxx (*M*), T-Rex (*M*), Tickle-me-Elmo (*M*), Tickle-me-Rihanna (*F*) Tomtom (*M*), Towie (*M/F*), Tron (*M*)

U – Ultravox (*M*), Urethra (*F*)

V – Van Halen (*M*), Veneria (*F*), Viagra (*F*), Vileda (*F*), Vinaigrette (*F*)

W – Walliam (*M*), Walmart (*M*), Wazza (*M*)

X – X-Box (*M/F*), Xena (*F*)

Y – Yakult (*M/F*)

Z – Zafira (*F*), Zinfandel (*M*), Zinfandella (*F*), Zod (*M*), Zumba (*F*)

CHILD TIMELINE
(OR CHILDLINE, FOR SHORT)

Your offspring's childhood is marked by distinctly different periods. The first of these is known as 'the terrible twos', when your child first begins to develop a sense of their place in the world and begins to push boundaries, often refusing to do as they are told. This is followed by the thoroughly unpleasant threes, the frightful fours, the forgettable fives, the soul-destroying sixes, the simply dreadful sevens, the excruciating eights, the nightmarish nines, the tiresome tens, the egregious elevens and the traumatic twelves. Then they're into their teens and things start to go downhill. My advice is just to sit tight and wait for it to pass. In another room. With a nice cup of tea. Or a bottle of gin.

FIRST WORDS

Often a baby's first word is 'Daddy', not 'Mummy'. This is because it's easier for it to express the letter 'D' than the letter 'M'. This needn't necessarily be the case, however. I found that a simple system of rewards and a mild course of electroshock treatment was all that was required to reverse this process. It's difficult to describe that heart-warming moment when your child's first word is 'Mummy' and you're able to remove the electrodes from his little chubby face – magical. Sadly, it doesn't work every time – the twins' first words were 'karaoke' and 'kebab'. Clearly, electricity has less effect on the letter 'k'.

FIRST STEPS

There is no moment to compare with the first time you see your baby take its first steps. All of a sudden, that once help-less bundle of bodily fluids is a toddler. You have to buy gates for the stairs, move your best crockery and hide the cat. What was once your domain is now a toy-strewn, juice-spattered nightmare. There are two ways to deal with this new, distress-ing situation – you can either make the mental and emotional adjustment to your new compromised family status, or you can move out. While the latter may seem attractive, it can be a costly and time-consuming process involving estate agents, removal men and social services. There is, however, a third approach which Stephen and I adopted, which was to have several more children as soon as possible. Not only does this increase your child benefit significantly, I find you can leave them all to take care of each other (in the broadest possible sense of the words 'take care'). This then frees you and your partner to enjoy life much the same as before, as long as you remember to check up on the little darlings once in a while. Every couple of months should be sufficient.

FIRST DAY AT SCHOOL

One of the most emotional moments in a parent's life is their child's first day at school. All of a sudden, that helpless bundle that spent all its time just lying on its back, burping and wet-ting itself is ready to make that momentous step – driving his child to school.

It can be a difficult time for the mother too. How will her little boy or girl cope? Will they be wary? Overwhelmed? Petrified? Will they join in with their classmates or spend all day crying to come home? It can be emotionally draining, sitting there, dunking your HobNob in your tea, expecting the phone to ring at any time with a call to come and fetch your child home. After a while, though, you realise that no such call will come and you can relax – you've got rid of them at last!

BEHAVIOUR

When it comes to your children's behaviour, teamwork is all-important. Whether rewarding or disciplining a child, the key is consistency; otherwise they will never learn right from wrong. In order to ensure this, it's important that both you and your partner work together. Some couples adopt a good cop/bad cop approach – Stephen prefers good cop/Robocop. I smile benignly whenever our children misbehave and he walks around in a metal suit shooting things. It seems to work. It's inherent in youngsters to want to push the boundaries you impose on them – it's all part of growing up but it can lead to confrontation, tantrums and tears. The answer to this is simple – if you don't give your children any boundaries, they have nothing to push!

Sibling rivalry can also be a big issue, particularly when you have more than one child. When a new baby arrives, the older brother or sister can often feel displaced from their parent's affections. To avoid this, the best thing is to make sure you don't give them any affection in the first place. That way, they will be perfectly well adjusted and have no such fears. Of course, it may not be just sibling rivalry you have to worry about. Often the father can feel usurped from his number one position in his wife's heart. This can lead to classic behaviour such as short temperedness, sulking and, in Stephen's case, hiring strippers. Again, the less affection you give them in the first place, the less they will be affected. Relationship experts refer to this as tough love, although I feel love may be too strong a word.

I do, however, feel that praise is over-rated when it comes to bringing up your children. It can lead to over-confidence and possibly arrogance when they grow older, plus there's nothing more unbearable than a mother relentlessly extolling their child's virtues against all evidence to the contrary. Even if your son or daughter should do something you deem praise-worthy, such as painting a pretty picture or composing a symphony, just carry on as if nothing has happened and before long, not only will they develop a true sense of their self-worth but they'll stop pestering you when you're trying to watch *Countdown*. Ignore some sense into them – that's what I say, dears.

Having said all this, you may find that, despite all of your best efforts, your little ones' behaviour may still be a cause for concern. Should this be the case, you may actually need to impose some kind of punishment. One popular sanction among child psychologists is the naughty step. This is where a child who has failed to meet your expectations for behaviour is forced to sit alone for a period of time on the staircase, the idea being that solitude allows them the opportunity to calm down and reflect on their behaviour, thereby leading to an improvement. There are pluses and minuses to this type of sanction – on the plus side, it saves you all that tedious telling them off and having to explain what they've done wrong but on the minus side, when you have a family of six or seven quite badly behaved children (plus an equally badly behaved husband) it can become unmanageable and quite difficult to get to the bathroom. Regardless of its drawbacks, I do find that this system can be successful up to a point so I've drawn up this step-by-naughty-step guide, or 12-step programme, beginning on the bottom step (which I have called step 1) for a minor offence and moving upwards according to the level of misdemeanour.

Step 1 – Not doing homework

Step 2 – Refusing to go to bed

Step 3 – Saying a naughty word

Step 4 – Saying a very naughty word

Step 5 – Saying one of Daddy's naughty words

Step 6 – Drawing on the wall

Step 7 – Shoplifting

Step 8 – Fraud

Step 9 – Arson

Step 10 – Third degree murder

Step 11 – Criticising their mother's cooking

Step 12 – Stephen's step

Conversely, a number of so-called child psychologists claim that some kind of reward scheme can be a valuable method of teaching your child right from wrong. I can't say that I subscribe to this theory personally, although on occasion I have found that 20 Benson & Hedges can keep them quiet while *Coronation Street*'s on. I've even tried positive reinforcement, which involves praising good behaviour. Unfortunately, this requires some form of good behaviour to praise and there are only so many days in the year. Alternatively, you can point out good behaviour in others in the hope that it will influence your child in a positive way but no matter how many times I say 'Look at that nice little girl. *She's* not stealing anyone's purse at knifepoint' I've still to detect any significant effect.

GENDER ROLES

This can be a tricky area and one which can cause conflict between a husband and wife. Personally, I have nothing against Stephen Junior dressing up like Liza Minnelli, as long as he's happy, but Stephen is far more traditional when it comes to gender roles. 'No son of mine is going to ...' is one of his favourite lines, variously followed by 'play tea parties', 'dress like a chorus girl' or 'give birth'. He refuses to let the boys play with dolls or the girls with books and if they're invited to fancy dress parties, he insists they wear what he calls gender-appropriate costumes – fireman or soldier for the boys, check-out assistant or stripper for the girls.

IMAGINARY FRIENDS

For a while I was convinced all of our six children had an imaginary friend until I realised we had seven children. I have to admit I was a little ashamed of this unforgivable oversight – I'd missed out on two years' child benefit.

HEALTH

All parents worry about their children's health but it's all too easy to become over-protective. Many scientists believe the dramatic rise in allergy-sufferers is down to our modern, sanitised lifestyle. These days children are brought up in a virtually germ-free environment thanks to advances in cleaning product advertising. Work surfaces are sterilised, floors are scrubbed until they shine and I believe in some homes, carpets are hoovered several times a year – madness!

Instead, in order to ensure our children grow up healthy and asthma-free, Stephen and I make sure they are exposed to as many strains of virus as possible, leaving kitchen surfaces and floors in their natural, encrusted state and arranging regular day-trips to maximum security government research laboratories and volunteering them for cosmetic testing whenever possible.

Even with such a comprehensive health strategy as this, your child may still succumb to the occasional cold. When this happens I simply prepare them a soothing cup of my own special Lemsoup, say 'there, there' and give them an extra blanket. If it's a particularly heavy cold, I sometimes even let them indoors. What mother could do more?

Another way to ensure the health of your little ones is through their diet. From the moment my children were born, I gave them only the very best food – Cot Noodle. It comes in a variety of delicious flavours and encourages bone growth and strong teeth. On special occasions, I even added boiling water. I spoil them, really I do.

As they get older, it can be more difficult to persuade your children to eat healthily. This is where you need to use a little imagination and creativity to make mealtimes more fun. One highly successful method I discovered was to stick sequins on their carrots and broccoli – I call it a 'vegazzle'.

SCHOOL REPORTS

Your child has just come running in from school, with a huge grin on their face, and a glowing school report clasped in their excited fist. But before you get too excited, I have one question for you ... What is that like? After more years of motherhood than I care to remember, I've only ever received two school reports – both from Hugh Junior who, unlike the rest of our brood, somehow seems to have escaped the Stephen gene altogether. Of course, I've rung the school to ask where the children's reports are but their responses range from 'Well, we gave it to them. Perhaps they lost it on the way home' to 'Who?'

If you are fortunate enough to receive your child's school report intact and stain-free, how should you react? My answer would be, with caution. Today's teachers lead a hectic, stress-ful life and they have no desire to increase this stress by provoking a pupil's parents. Very often the slightest thing can influence what they write about your child — their father holding the entire staff hostage in a stock cupboard and forcing them to listen to Michael Bolton, to give one completely random example.

In order to avoid such totally-imagined-for-the-sake-of-argument confrontations as this, teachers have perfected a language of their own, not dissimilar to 'office speak' where the true meaning is submerged in a sea of indecipherable gobbledegook. To help you interpret your child's report, here is a short Teacher-to-Parent translation guide. For no reason other than ease of understanding, I've inserted my own children's names into the example phrases.

Stephen Junior pays close attention to woodwork —
He enjoys licking the window frames

Asbo has engaged in a number of scientific activities —
One is a number

Viennetta has completed the R.E. curriculum satisfactorily —
She may have turned up once or twice. It doesn't really matter — it's not a real subject, is it?

Subo has an enthusiastic attitude to learning —
She runs around the classroom making train noises

Stephen Junior has an enquiring mind —
He keeps asking to go to the toilet

Brangelina is a challenging child —
She keeps challenging the other children to fights. And the teachers. And the police.

KEEPING THEM ENTERTAINED

This is one of the rare few areas of parenthood on which Stephen and I disagree. While, generally, I believe that they should be left to amuse themselves wherever possible, Stephen loves entertaining our children. Only last week he kept them enthralled for hours, making balloon animals. Eventually the helium canister ran out but the kids still had hours of fun trying to get the cat and gerbils down from the ceiling. And he likes nothing better than a rainy Sunday afternoon indoors playing games with them. Poker's his favourite because, as he says, it's not only fun but profitable (it's also the reason we use the term 'lend' rather than 'give' pocket money), although he's equally happy to play Which Raindrop Will Reach the Bottom of the Window Pane First or Hungry Hippos.

Occasionally I join in too, provided I'm not already occupied with cooking Sunday lunch or doing the washing up after Sunday lunch or complaining that Stephen never does the washing up after Sunday lunch, although I prefer board games as they're a true family experience – plenty of squabbling and competitive violence. Like most households, after years of use most of our games have the odd item missing but we've managed to combine the remaining pieces to create the perfect family game – Trivial Cluedopolobblextric. We even had a few random extra bits left over so we made another game – we called it Mouse Trap, although we don't play that very often as it takes ages to set up and only a few minutes to play. Although it is quite good at catching mice.

CHAPTER SEVEN

Getting Away From It All

HOBBIES AND PASTIMES

In TODAY's world, it's important to take a little time every now and again to smell the roses – or anything other than soiled nappies and stale kebabs. It's all too easy for the modern married couple to fill their lives with work and forget to allow time for leisure. This could be in the form of a hobby or pastime, maybe a craft or a sport, possibly a night school course of some description – it doesn't really matter what it is as long as you do it separately. In the early days of our marriage I made the mistake of enrolling Stephen and myself on a pottery course together. Unfortunately, he had only recently seen *Ghost* and we were asked to leave.

THE SHED

This is why the shed is such a crucial element of the matrimonial home. Without it, a husband would have to smoke in the house, read his dubious magazines in the house and, simply, spend more time in the house. In truth, I haven't the faintest idea what Stephen gets up to in his shed and I don't want to know, provided it doesn't involve too many women or fire-arms. I'm just glad to have him out from under my feet. Without it, he'd be stuck on the sofa all hours of the day between last orders and opening time.

GENEALOGY

One hobby I've taken up recently is genealogy – the study of your family tree. Although I have to say Stephen's is more like a forest – not dissimilar to the one in *The Wizard of Oz*. My interest was awakened by television programmes such as *Don't You Know Who I Am?*, in which minor celebrities trace their ancestral roots and cry a lot.

By contrast, I find the process thoroughly uplifting. It's fascinating to discover what various generations of my family did for a living. For example, in the early 20th century, my Great Aunt Agatha left the country to find employment in Hollywood. Apparently, she worked behind the scenes on a number of specialist, low-budget productions. I'm not entirely sure what her job entailed (so many of these film industry occupations have odd names such as 'best boy' and 'grip') but according to my research she was employed as a fluffer. Sadly, she soon returned to England so I assume she never made it big.

AMATEUR DRAMATICS

Another interest of mine is the stage and, while I could never hope to do anything on a professional basis given my family commitments, I gain a great deal of pleasure from my association with our local amateur dramatic group, 'Curtains for Oscar'. They specialise in the works of one of my favourite playwrights, Oscar Wilde, and I was delighted to be given the starring role of Lady Blenkinsopp in an acclaimed performance of his rarely-seen unfinished play about the exorcism of a young girl, *Whatever Possessed Her?* For those unfamiliar with piece, I have reproduced a scene from the final act for your enjoyment and education.

LADY BLENKINSOPP: Certainly the young gentleman to whom you refer does appear to have turned my god-niece's head somewhat. Somewhat more than 360 degrees unless I'm very much mistaken. Desist immediately, Millicent. You know how I disapprove of such revolutionary activity.

MILLICENT: Blaaarrgghh! (*sound of vomiting*) Your mother cuts frocks in Hull!

LADY BLENKINSOPP: Oh my word, I feel quite faint. Come down from the ceiling at once, Millicent! A lady should never rise above her station ... or her bedstead. What is the meaning of this unseemly behaviour?

MILLICENT: I'm terribly sorry, my dearest god-auntie. I know not what ails me. Perchance, I have a touch of the influenza?

CEDRIC: I think that, perhaps, Lady Blenkinsopp, I may be in a position to furnish you with an explanation of sorts for Miss Arbuthnot's somewhat unconventional demeanour.

LADY BLENKINSOPP: Then do so immediately, Mr deAlgernon, before my god-niece sees fit to propel her partially-digested elevenses upon my bosom a further time.

CEDRIC: I am very much distressed, madam, to admit that on the evening of October the 25th, I found myself on the platform of Victoria station. The northern line.

LADY BLENKINSOPP: The line is immaterial.

CEDRIC: And it was while waiting for the 7:38 to Norfolk that my eye was caught by a particularly well-endowed, partially-dressed young lady, casually propelling about her wrist a small leather handbag of Eastern European origin.

LADY BLENKINSOPP: A hand ... ?

CEDRIC (*interrupting*): Indeed. So, being a true gentleman, I approached her and offered her my coat ... and sixteen shillings and thruppence.

LADY BLENKINSOPP: Am I to assume from this tiresome preamble that the young lady of whom you speak was a female of somewhat easy virtue?

CEDRIC: I am very much ashamed to say that she was, Lady Blenkinsopp, and that we engaged in an act of a prurient nature in the left luggage office.

LADY BLENKINSOPP: My dear fellow. Are you incompletely sane? I trust that was the extent of your indiscretion.

CEDRIC: Absolutely. Completely. That is, until an additional young lady proceeded to join us in what I believe is commonly referred to in modern parlance as a threesome?

LADY BLENKINSOPP: A threesome? In my day, a gentle-man considered himself extremely fortunate to engage in a onesome, and then only on public holidays. Mr deAlgernon, to engage in carnal activity with one prostitute can be regarded as a misfortune, to engage with two looks like per-version – a quality to be very much admired in the modern gentleman. And is it a preconception to suppose that a pro-phylactic was deployed on this occasion?

CEDRIC: It is, and indeed was, very much a pre-conception, Lady Blenkinsopp. Alas, one of the ladies fell with child that very evening, although I very much regret to say that I know not which, and so, while I remain very definitely your god-niece's father it pains me to say that the identity of her mother remains a mystery. So, not wishing the dear, unfortunate child to suffer the torment and ignominy of a cruel society, I did what any right thinking and loyal father would do, I put her up for adoption. A lovely gentleman – a Mr Lucifus J Beelze-beast.

LADY BLENKINSOPP: Well, I am relieved to hear that, at least. And is that the end of the story?

CEDRIC: Absolutely, my dear Lady Blenkinsopp. Unless you count the lovely young lady I accidentally met by the docks this morning. But that was merely for the administering of manual relief.

LADY BLENKINSOPP: A hand ... ?

Unfortunately, the play ends at this point, poor Oscar unable to complete it due to ill-fitting trousers. Being a keen and not untalented wordsmith, I offered to supply the remaining lines myself but, try as I might, I simply couldn't imagine what Lady Blenkinsopp's next word may have been and so, I'm afraid, it remains unfinished.

However, despite my inability to conclude the work, the attempt did re-awaken my literary ambitions and I proceeded to create my very own piece for the group to perform. It was a play loosely based on my own experiences and one which, if I say so myself, was received with incredulity by its one and only audience. In fact, I was so pleased with it, I even sent the script to several Hollywood studios but as of yet I haven't heard back from any of them (I imagine this is what other screenwriters call 'development hell'). As I suspect it could be several months before you are afforded the opportunity to see the movie for yourself, here is what I believe they call in the trade, a little teaser ...

WHEN EDNA MET STEPHEN (AGAIN)

A warm summer evening. Edna has just paid Stephen's bail following his arrest for persistent ukulele-playing and telling girls on the Spiffing Burberry railway station platform to smile. They enter a small, insalubrious kebab shop.

STEPHEN: Thank you. No-one's ever been so kind to me before.
EDNA: I understand.
STEPHEN: Understand what?
EDNA: Oh, nothing.
STEPHEN: What?
EDNA: Forget about it, dear.

STEPHEN: Forget about what?

EDNA: It's not important, really.

STEPHEN: Just tell me.

EDNA: Well, it's just that you obviously haven't had a good friend before.

STEPHEN: Yes I have.

EDNA: I don't think you have, dear.

STEPHEN: It just so happens that I have had plenty of good friends!

EDNA: Really? Who, may I ask?

STEPHEN: What?

EDNA: With whom did you have these wonderful friend-ships?

STEPHEN: I ... I ... I'm not going to tell you!

EDNA: Fine, dear. Don't tell me.

KEBAB SHOP OWNER: Hello, my friend. What can I get for you?

STEPHEN: See? Here's one.

EDNA: Really? And what's his name?

STEPHEN: (*long pause*) ... Kebab Shop ... Man

EDNA: Ah.

STEPHEN: Anyway, I'll have the King Kong Kebab with chilli sauce and garlic mayonnaise and large chips.

KEBAB SHOP OWNER: One King Kong and chips for my good friend, Mr Stephen.

STEPHEN: But I'd like the meat shaved from the top of the lump and I don't want the garlic mayonnaise all over, I want it on the side and I'd like naan bread instead of pitta bread if you have it if not then no garlic mayo just regular mayo but only if it's real if it's salad cream otherwise nothing.

KEBAB SHOP OWNER: Not even the chips?

STEPHEN: No, just the chips, but no vinegar.

KEBAB SHOP OWNER: Oh ... kay, whatever you say, Mr Stephen.

EDNA: You're a very unusual person.

STEPHEN: Thank you.

EDNA: It wasn't a compliment.

STEPHEN: Are you sure?

EDNA: Well, maybe just a little ...

STEPHEN: I knew it – you were chatting me up!

EDNA: I most certainly was not! Can't a woman say a man is unusual without it being a chat-up line? In that case I take it back.

STEPHEN: You can't take it back.

EDNA: Why not?

STEPHEN: Because I can't hear you taking it back ... (*he sticks his fingers in his ears*) La-la-la-la-la ... See?

EDNA: Oh good grief.

STEPHEN: (*taking his fingers out of his ears and licking one*) So are we going to sleep together now? I mean after the kebab, of course.

EDNA: Certainly not! We can never do ... you-know-what.

STEPHEN: You-know-which?

EDNA: You-know-exactly-what.

STEPHEN: Oh, you-know-that!

EDNA: Precisely.

STEPHEN: But why not? It wouldn't mean anything.

EDNA: My dear man, men and women can never do you-know-what without it meaning anything because the friendship part always gets in the way.

STEPHEN: That's not true, I've done it hundreds of times

and there's never been any friendship involved.

EDNA: No you haven't.

STEPHEN: Yes I have.

EDNA: You most certainly have not.

STEPHEN: Yes I have.

EDNA: You only think you have.

STEPHEN: You're saying I was friends with all those women without knowing it?

EDNA: No, what I'm saying is they all wanted to be friends with you. Though heavens only knows why.

STEPHEN: They did not!

EDNA: I'm afraid they did, dear.

STEPHEN: They did not!

EDNA: They did indeed.

STEPHEN: How do you know?

EDNA: Because no woman can have meaningless you-know-what with a man she finds ... unusual. She always wants to be friends with him.

STEPHEN: So you're saying that a woman can have meaningless 'you-know-what' with a man she finds ... usual?

EDNA: No, you pretty much want to be friends with them too.

STEPHEN: What if they don't want to be friends with you?

EDNA: It doesn't matter because the friendship thing is already out there so the you-know-what is ultimately doomed and that, my dear, is the end of the story.

STEPHEN: Well I guess we're not going to be doing it then.

EDNA: Correct.

STEPHEN: That's too bad. I've just started wearing my summer pants. And the other night I made love to this woman, and it was so incredible that I took her to a place that wasn't human. She actually mooed.

EDNA: You made a woman moo? (*Stephen raises his forefingers to his head to simulate horns and bellows like a bull*) Oh, dear lord.

STEPHEN: You're telling me no-one's ever made you moo?

EDNA: Certainly not.

STEPHEN: Low a little ... ?

EDNA: Don't be disgusting.

STEPHEN: So what do you do, exactly? With your ... gentleman friends.

EDNA: Not that it's any of your business, I'm sure, but I generally take them to an art gallery. Or glass-blowing factory. Then perhaps a tea room. Nothing like this place. (*smiles at the kebab shop owner*) No offence, Mr Man, dear.

KEBAB SHOP OWNER: None taken, my friend.

STEPHEN: And do you think they have a good time?

EDNA: Of course they do.

STEPHEN: How do you know?

EDNA: What do you mean how do I know? I know.

STEPHEN: Are you sure?

EDNA: What are you saying, that they pretend to enjoy it?

STEPHEN: It's possible.

EDNA: Don't be ridiculous!

STEPHEN: Why? Most men at one time or another have pretended to enjoy themselves. If they're after ... you-know-what.

EDNA: Well they haven't pretended to enjoy themselves with me.

STEPHEN: How do you know?

EDNA: I just do.

STEPHEN: Are you absolutely sure?

EDNA: I think I would have noticed if they had appeared to be enjoying themselves.

STEPHEN: Ah, at last ...

(*the kebab shop owner places Stephen's kebab on the counter in front of him. Stephen immediately starts to devour it, ferociously*)

STEPHEN: Mmm ... Oh ... Mmmm ...

EDNA: Are you quite alright, dear?

STEPHEN: Oh ... Oh god ... Mmmm Oh God ... Mmmm ... mmm ... mmmm ... Oh God ... Oh yeah, that's so good ... (*Edna shuffles uneasily and looks nervously around the kebab shop*)

EDNA: What on earth are you doing, dear? People are looking.

STEPHEN: Mmmmm ... Yes Yes Yes... Mmm ... mmm ... Yes Yes Yes ... Mmm ... Mmmm ... Mmmmm ... Oh God Oh ... Huh?

KEBAB SHOP OWNER: (*turning to Edna*) And what would you like, my friend?

EDNA: Well, I'm certainly not having what he's having!

DAY TRIPS AND HOLIDAYS

For those of you seeking to escape those four walls but unable to free yourself of your familial responsibilities, a day trip or family holiday might be the answer. These come in all shapes and forms – the only limitation being your imagination. And your budget. And whether or not your children suffer from travel sickness.

Picnics

What more enjoyable way can there be for a family to spend time together than to go for a lovely picnic? Eating al fresco is one of the greatest pleasures in life, laying a blanket on the ground in a beautiful golden meadow, sipping champagne and breaking bread together as you listen to the birdsong and bathe in the glorious summer sun – idyllic! Unless you live in Britain, of course. Here is my recipe for a traditional British picnic.

In days gone by, the great British family picnic was a commonplace, almost daily event – until houses were invented. In the Edwardian era, the picnic was a very grand affair featuring tables, butlers and lobster aplenty. These days, things are a little less extravagant but no less enjoyable.

First you need a hamper, or other appropriate food-carrying receptacle such as a cool-box or small suitcase. Preparation is everything when it comes to picnics – make sure you begin at least half an hour before you head out. Pack whatever cutlery you will need. Don't worry about the family silver-effect – plastic knives, forks, spoons and beakers are perfectly acceptable. If space is at a premium you can even take multipurpose items such as the spork (a combination of spoon and fork) or a relatively recent scientific picnic advancement, a clever combination of wine glass, tankard, goblet and cup – the Wankard 'n' Goblup.

Of course, no picnic would be complete without that all-important flask of tea. Simply follow my patented Perfect Cuppa recipe from earlier in the book, adjusting the number of teabags to account for the number of picnickers. Again, if space is at a premium, instead of the standard size tartan family flask, you can use a smaller, slimmer steel hip flask, making sure you first empty the contents down your throat.

The next stage is to decide where you are going to go. This is always a difficult decision for us as McDonalds and KFC are in opposite directions. Generally, after a lively family discussion, we end up going to both. You should never skimp when it comes to picnics!

Once the burgers, nuggets, drumsticks, fries and Alvin and the Chipmunks figurines are safely in your hamper, you are ready to hit the open road and go off into the wild grey yonder. If you intend to use an official picnic site, make sure you park within a short distance of the tables. That way, you have something to look at through the windows while you eat your food.

Other possible picnic venues you may wish to consider are the sea front, Tesco's car park and that old stand-by, the lay-by (please remember that the hard shoulder on a motorway should only be used for an emergency picnic). All of these venues allow for a thoroughly enjoyable family picnic without the inconvenience of having to leave your vehicle.

For those of you brave enough to attempt a meal in the Not-so-great Outdoors, you have more than the British Summer to contend with. While we may not have the same picnicking concerns as our friends across the Atlantic, such as grizzly bears and drive-by shootings, there are still those old enemies of the al frescan, the cow-pat and our little six-legged friend, the ant.

The humble ant is an extraordinary creature, capable of lifting up to six billion times its own bodyweight – the equivalent of you or I lifting an oil tanker or an ant lifting a house. To the ant, a picnic isn't a family occasion, it's a finely tuned military operation, where the objective is to free as many items of food from the enemies' clutches as quickly as possible. If you are to stand a chance of enjoying a peaceful family picnic, you must take extreme measures. When we last encountered this problem, Stephen tried winning the hearts and minds of the local ant population by handing out Britney Spears CDs and posing for photographs with them but to no avail, so he was left with no choice but to adopt what he calls 'Shock and Awe' tactics. Essentially, this involves him removing his trousers and dancing the Macarena until the other picnickers can't take any more, leaving us to sit at whichever ant-free picnic table we choose (CAUTIONARY NOTE – if you choose to adopt this approach, be aware that the conflict could continue for several years, sustaining many casualties).

Camping and Caravanning

If you prefer to get a real taste of the wild outdoors, as opposed to the wild indoors, you can always try camping or caravanning. Just pause for a moment to picture yourself, your partner and your children spending the night together under canvas – and buy a caravan. You just can't beat the thrill of setting off into the wild, caravan careering hazardously as you round each tight bend in that country road until, finally, you arrive at your destination and experience that inimitable adrenalin rush as you pitch up for the night and open the caravan door to discover which of your cooking utensils and children are still intact.

The Family Holiday

Of all the different types of holiday, Stephen's favourite is the 'staycation', or as we call it in Great Britain, the 'brollyday'. He has all the amenities of being at home without the inconvenience of travelling, meeting other people and having to eat foreign curries and kebabs. On the odd occasion I have managed to persuade him to leave this sceptred isle, one of the difficulties we've faced is conversing with the locals. This can be doubly challenging if they don't speak English. To this end, Stephen has developed his own particular language, Desperanto, which, when spoken loudly enough with enough accompanying hand gestures, seems to make him understood. Here is a list of his top 10 – indeed, his only 10 – all-purpose phrases, seemingly understandable in every corner of the northern Mediterranean. Personally, I haven't a clue what they mean.

1. O sole mio
2. Una paloma blanca
3. Vorsprung durch technik
4. Hasta la vista, baby
5. Fan dabi dozi

6. Milli vanilli
7. Zig a zig ah
8. Julio Iglesias
9. Va va voom
10. Nessun dorma

If you would like further information about family holidays abroad, I recommend you purchase a copy of the excellent *How To Have An Almost Perfect Family Holiday*. I forget the author's name ...

CHAPTER EIGHT

Magic Moments

WEDDING ANNIVERSARIES

T RADITIONALLY, each year of your marriage is cele-
brated with a different theme. Most people know about
gold, silver and ruby but here is a comprehensive list I've
compiled with the assistance of Vaguelytruepedia.com.

---

1. Milk
2. Velcro
3. MDF
4. Lint
5. Cubic Zirconium
6. Fibreglass
7. Tupperware
8. Meat
9. Lego
10. Nectar Points
11. Key Ring
12. Cheese
13. Socks

---

14. Oregano

15. Meccano

16. Garage Flowers

17. Tattoo

18. A Nice Cardigan

19. Phone Credit

20. Bodyshop Stuff

21. Gin

22. Earth, Wind and Fire

23. Cash

24. Penguin Adoption Certificate

25. Silver

26. Disney

27. Petrol

28. Polyester

29. Kryptonite

30. 2−4−1 Gift Token to Alton Towers

31. Peat

32. Just a Card

33. Cinzano

34. Beige

35. Andrew Lloyd-Webber

36. Laser Eye Surgery

37. Buck-A-Roo

38. Scalextric

39. Plasticene

40. Ruby

41. Bubblewrap

42. A surprise

43. DVD Box Set
44. Daniel O'Donnell CD
45. Jigsaw Puzzle
46. Batteries
47. iPhone
48. Tattoo Removal
49. Ovaltine
50. Gold

Wedding anniversaries can be difficult occasions. To celebrate one properly can take weeks of preparation and years of being married to someone. Of course, even the most meticulous preparation can't guarantee that everything will run smoothly. One tiny thing can still ruin the occasion – generally the husband. Even my own marriage, perfect though it is, has suffered the occasional hiccup.

One year, I decided to give Stephen a big anniversary surprise. I constructed a huge cake, reminiscent of the one we had for our wedding – only this time it would contain me and not a stripper. It was a monumental creation, standing fully six feet high. It took weeks to make, using eight metres of marzipan, 12 bowls of icing, plus a fair bit of cardboard and several steel joists (more than I usually use when baking a cake, at any rate). Despite its great size I managed to conceal it from Stephen by hiding it somewhere I knew he would never look – the kitchen.

Finally, on the day of our anniversary, after sending Stephen to the corner shop for a pint of milk, I wheeled it out into the living room and carefully climbed inside, ready to leap out and surprise him when he returned. As an extra romantic touch I had also put on my wedding dress (which, I'm proud to say, still fits perfectly – partly due to my having been eight months pregnant with Stephen Junior at the time). And so, with all the preparations in place, I crouched down in the dark, breathing as quietly as I could, and waited.

And waited.

And waited.

What happened next is best illustrated by an extract from my diary…

Wednesday

I woke with a start. I'd been having that dream about being buried alive, only this time it was me, not Stephen, so I was sweating and shaking. I blinked. It was pitch black. Where was I? What was that scratching sound? Had I really been buried alive? My mind did somersaults until at last I remembered. I was sitting in my wedding dress inside a giant cake. Obviously. I must have fallen asleep. What time was it? I twisted my arm awkwardly and pressed the light button on the Thomas the Tank Engine digital watch Stephen bought me for our last anniversary. 3:28 AM.

I froze. There was that scratching sound again. Only louder this time. And accompanied by some sort of strange humming. Then it stopped. Then there was the sound of something metal falling onto stone. Then swearing. Then the scratching sound again. And finally a key being rammed into the lock and turning. The doorknob rattled for several minutes – I keep telling him to fix that – before finally, heavy feet fell through the door.

'Surprise.'

Stephen stared blankly at me, standing in a giant cake, jam stains on my face, crumbs down my lace dress and hands on my hips.

After what seemed like an eternity, a broad grin flashed across his face and he held out a half-empty carton of milk.

'Surprise!' he replied, before collapsing onto the sofa.

I glared in silence at his giggling, disheveled form. I suppose it was my fault for giving him my purse. I should have known he would take it straight to the Dog & Duck, and then – judging by the robot dance he was now attempting to recreate – on to that stupid sci-fi-theme nightclub, Outer Space. I sighed. There was no talking to him when he was like this. And so, I resorted to the only language he understands after 15 Lime and Kiwi Bacardi Breezers ... Karaoke.

'I felt I was a fraud – I was petrified,
Kept thinking I could never eat without you, Stephen Fry.
But then I cooked so many meals
While you were boozing down the pub,
And I grew cross,
And now I couldn't give a toss.

And so you're back
From Outer Space,
With your trousers round your ankles and that daft look
    upon your face.
I shouldn't have worn this stupid frock,
I should have sat and watched TV,
If I had known for just one second,
    you'd be back at half past three.

Go on now, go! Walk out the door!
Just turn the knob hard,
'Cause it's not working any more.
Weren't you the one who had the gall to criticise?
Did you eat my crumble?
Did you eat my peach and tuna pie?
No more, not I,
I will serve five!
Oh, as long as I know how to cook,
I know they'll stay alive.
I've got all our kids to feed,
And I've got all the Spam I need,
And I'll serve five,
I will serve five ... or is it six?

It takes all the strength I have,
Not to stand and rant,
Or stuff this ham and lemon pizza down your underpants.
And I spent oh so many nights,
Just eating dinner by myself.
I used to sob,
Instead of cutting off your ... privileges.

And you see me?
I'm over here.
I'm not that hat stand in the corner,
You've had too much beer.
And so you felt like crawling home
And just expect me to be free.
Now I'm saving all my cooking for someone

who'll eat their tea!
Go on now, go!'

And so he went …

In the plant pot. And the sink. And the wardrobe.

And I went straight to bed, dabbing my streaming mascara with my marzipan-covered veil.

Thursday

I can never stay angry with Stephen for long. No matter what he's done, somehow he always manages to come up with that romantic gesture that melts my heart and reminds me why I married him all those years ago. This morning, when I slammed the fridge door after replacing the milk for my morning cup of tea, I saw them. 13 randomly-coloured magnetic letters, spelling out the words YOU COMPLETE ME. My body flooded immediately with warm, tingling emotion and helplessly, I rushed upstairs to give him a huge kiss. After I'd finished my cup of tea.

Friday

Found two magnetic letter S's on the kitchen floor. Must have fallen off when I slammed the fridge door. Oh well.

BIRTHDAYS

Birthdays can be a joyous occasion – for a child. But a child's birthday party can be a highly stressful and exhausting event for the parents, especially if you choose to host it in your own home. Your house can be like a cross between London Zoo and a Monster Truck Rally with screaming kids chasing about, flinging food and throwing up all over the place but you still need to get it ready for the party. There are balloons to blow up, banners to hang and a cake to bake. On top of that, you need to plan party games, buy prizes and send out invitations. Food-wise, you can't go wrong with the old favourites – crisps, sausage rolls, jelly and ice cream, fizzy pop and a large bucket.

In addition, some parents choose to book a children's entertainer. We normally have Les – he's great with the kids. He paints their faces, performs magic tricks and even puts on a little puppet show. It really takes the pressure off us as, within half an hour, most of the guests have run home screaming and we can enjoy a relatively peaceful party. Then all you have to worry about is waiting for the parents to pick up the remaining children. Inevitably, there will always be one flustered mother or father who turns up half an hour late full of apologies but don't worry – if you're lucky, they'll take one of yours by mistake.

Fortunately, these days there are many alternatives to the home party – if it's your daughter's birthday you could opt for a catwalk party, where she and her friends can spend a delightful couple of hours in the latest fashions, taking it in turns to walk a cat. Your son, on the other hand, may prefer something more energetic, like Laser Quest or inner-city rioting. And of course, there's always the easy option – a visit to the local cinema. This can be a relatively inexpensive and stress-free way to spend a few hours before returning home to see what kind of mess all those children have been making at the party.

CHRISTMAS

Christmas is one of the most stressful times a couple can experience, second only to moving house and the honeymoon. More marriages break up over the festive period than at any other time. For this reason, my advice would be, just relax and enjoy it, dears. However, if you insist on keeping your marriage intact here are a few tried and trusted tips to help you survive Christmas.

Father Christmas

This is the big one, dears. Eventually, no matter what you do, your children will inevitably reach that difficult age – the age when they start to believe in Father Christmas (or Santa Claus, as our charming American cousins call him). Despite your best efforts to deny his existence, there will always be some smart Alec school friend who insists on ruining it for everyone by telling them Father Christmas exists. Millions of weak parents find themselves succumbing to social pressure and end up spending a small fortune on presents to appease their little ones. I'm ashamed to say that even we have fallen foul of this scurrilous conspiracy, sometimes spending upwards of £30 on gifts – which equates to very nearly £5 per child.

Of course, we've tried taking them along to see department store Santas, pointing out their ill-fitting beards and whisky breath. We've blocked up our chimney. Stephen's even not dressed up in a red suit on Christmas Eve, but all to no avail. No matter what we do, our children simply refuse to let go of the captivating and magical concept of free stuff.

The Tree

No family yuletide would be complete without the all-important Christmas tree. It's a focal point for the festive season – we place presents beneath it, we gather round it to sing carols and we all hop about cursing it when we tread on its needles in our bare feet. Another annual tradition in the Fry household is something we call the 'getting of the tree'. This isn't as straightforward as it sounds. Most families buy their Christmas trees from garden centres, supermarkets or their local grocery store but Stephen, being a typical Neanderthal hunter-gatherer (and a bit of a cheapskate), prefers to cut down his own. A couple of weeks before Christmas he'll head boldly out into the night, chainsaw in hand and balaclava over his face, in search of the perfect tree. I have to admit I do find it difficult to sleep, knowing Stephen is out all alone in the dead of night with only a chainsaw to protect him, but every year he returns safe and sound and when we wake up the following morning, there it is, standing proudly in the living room - a magnificent, tall, bushy specimen, branches miraculously hung with baubles and lights and a gleaming star on the top. I can honestly say it's the best Christmas tree in town – and has been for the past six years that the one in the marketplace has been stolen, although I simply can't begin to imagine who would do such a thing.

Mistletoe

Now, I'm as fond of Christmas decorations and traditions as the next woman but I'm afraid I do have to draw the line at mistletoe. If you have a husband like Stephen, it's just asking for a trouble, believe me. If it weren't bad enough that he always hangs it over the front door and gives a sloppy, wet Christmas kiss to every woman who comes within 100 yards of it, he insists on calling it 'first base'. He also hangs up a sprig of holly, which he calls 'second base' and the ivy is 'third base'. As for the Christmas wreath – well, all I can say is the lady from the Salvation Army still hasn't fully recovered. It's no wonder he's banned from Interflora.

Presents

As if the pressure of catering for family and friends weren't enough, there's the small matter of Christmas presents. It's difficult enough trying to find meaningless fripperies to give people you barely know but buying gifts for your spouse and children can be even harder – after all, you're far more likely to see them again before next Christmas so there will be plentiful opportunities for them to display their disappointment. In the children's case this can manifest itself in sulking and stomping around loudly. In Stephen's case, much the same, only sulkier and louder.

Nowadays, thanks to the internet, it's perfectly possible to do your entire Christmas shopping from the comfort of your own armchair. It's my opinion, however, that while this is terribly convenient, it isn't really getting into the Christmas spirit. Online stores providing lists of personalised gift suggestions may be terribly helpful, but where on earth is the fun in that? To my mind, it can never really replace that disappointed look on the recipient's face. Also, what's Christmas without a little festive bloodshed?

For those of you less inclined to commercial violence, the toy shops and department stores provide a list of 'this year's must-have toys' for your little ones. This is a very helpful marketing ploy as it inevitably leads to panic buying for these highly sought-after items, leaving the rest of the less-desired toys for everyone else to buy at their leisure. If, however, you enjoy engaging in this annual ritual of violence and mayhem, here is this year's top ten:

1. *Tracey Island* – Tracey Emin's unmade island, surrounded by a sea of bodily fluids, used condoms and bewildered lookers-on. Thought-provoking and oodles of fun!

2. *Buck-A-Rooney* – load up the cuddly Premiership footballer with as many personal problems as you can before he lashes out wildly. Deluxe edition comes with eagle eyes and fairly realistic hair.

3. *Kids' Cabbage Patches* – for the child in your family who just can't shake that addiction to their five-a-day.

4. *Hungry Hippies* – how many brownies can you shove down your hippy's mouth at three o'clock in the morning?

5. *XXX-Box* – the latest console for the solo player – complete with a range of games including *Call of Booty*, *Mario Bothers* and *Sonic the Crack-whore*.

6. *Tiny Tears* – an empty box.

7. *Builder Bare* – can the cuddly construction worker complete a whole shift without his trousers falling completely down?

8. *Nintendoggers* – crazy car chaos for everyone! For 2–16 players, depending on the size of your vehicle.

9. *Connect 2* – for the ADHD-sufferer in your family.

10. *My Little Penis* – every girl's best friend. Comes in a variety of shapes and colours. Collect 'em all!

While shopping for your children can be a challenge, buying a gift for your husband or wife can be even trickier. The important thing to remember is, no matter how long you've been married, how many wonderful moments you've shared, whatever you do, keep the receipt. That way you can both go out on Boxing Day and exchange it for something you actually want. It takes the worry out of Christmas shopping, guarantees your loved one gets what they really want and means you don't need to waste hours looking around for that perfect gift. Or even, vaguely acceptable gift. Unfortunately, my Stephen loses receipts like he loses winning betting slips and after years of disappointment and garage flowers, I finally had to bite the bullet and tell him to be more original. To be fair to him, he took me at my word and last year he genuinely surprised me with that *Adopt a Snow Leopard* gift pack. It was so nice that he actually put a little thought into my present for once, although you should see the state of the curtains. Fortunately, it was part of an exchange programme and I understand the twins are causing Twycross Zoo a great deal more trouble.

The Days Before Christmas

So with Christmas Day approaching and excitement building, how do you keep your impat t little 'darlings' occupied? Fortunately, there are a number f festive family options available, including an increasing number of Christmas-themed attractions up and down the country.

One of our favourites is Yellowsnow Park, a wonderful yuletide experience constructed every December in the Dog & Duck car park. Our kids just love it. As the promotional pamphlet says, 'Laugh along with your little ones as they shoot down our Winter Olympic-style luge track on a beer tray at 60 miles per hour, doing their best to avoid the oncoming vehicles! Thrill as they try to escape the clutches of our very own abominable snowman, Hairy Geoff! And see their little faces light up as they enjoy their complementary Benson and Hedges from Santa!'.

Another time-consuming treat is the traditional British pantomime although, personally, I have to say I've never seen the attraction of watching a man dressed as a woman spouting all kinds of ridiculous advice for comic effect. Stephen seems to enjoy them for some reason, bless him – possibly because it's the only time he's allowed to shout out in a public place without breaching the terms of his court order.

The Night Before Christmas

You're almost there. Just one more hurdle to complete – getting your children to sleep on Christmas Eve. However, this can be a real challenge, if they are anything like ours – bubbling to the brim with a potent cocktail of anticipation, excitement, nervous energy and potent cocktails. This new-fangled social media thingummy doesn't help either, what with them staying up until the early hours messaging their friends and poking complete strangers. It's no wonder their little minds are still racing when their heads hit the pillow.

After years of tears, tantrums and tweets I finally came up with the solution – send Stephen to the pub. However, this still left me having to deal with the children's tears, tantrums and tweets so I came up with a further solution. Being a writer of not inconsiderable note, it was a relatively simple task for me to come up with something to shake the sugar-plums out of their heads and teach them the true meaning of Christmas. Now every year at bedtime, I tell them to turn off their computers and mobile phones and I read them the following poem. By the time I've finished, they're usually so exhausted or terrified they shoot straight up to bed without a word. It's a simple cautionary tale, although I can't for the life of me think what inspired the main character ...

How the Frynch Stole Twitmas

Every Twit down in Twitville
Liked Twitter a lot,
But the Frynch,
Who lived just North of London,
Did NOT!

The Frynch hated Twitter!
The whole Twitmas season.
Now please don't ask why,
No-one quite knows the reason.

It could be his laptop
Wasn't plugged in quite right,
It could be perhaps
That his pants were too tight.

But I think the most likely reason of all,
May have been that his dongle was two sizes too small.

Whatever the reason,
His dongle or pants,
He stared at the screen,
Having one of his rants.

'They're tweeting their greetings!'
He started to shake.
'Tomorrow is Twitmas,
This is too much to take!'

Then he growled, with his Frynch fingers
    nervously drumming,
'I MUST find a way to keep Twitmas from coming!'

For tomorrow he knew all those twittering nerds,
Would wake bright and early, like little blue birds
And the words! The words!

Oh, the words, words, words, words!
That's the thing that he hated!
  The WORDS, WORDS, WORDS, WORDS!

For the Twits young and old would sit down on their seats,
And they'd tweet. And they'd tweet. And they'd
  TWEET, TWEET, TWEET, TWEET!

And the more the Frynch thought of this whole Twitmas row,
The more the Frynch thought, 'I must stop Twitter now!
Why for more than three years, I've put up with this crap.
I must stop Twitter from working – Asap!'

Then he got an idea!
A devilish idea!
More devilish than anything got in Ikea!

And he grabbed some bin bags
And some old empty cases,
(He just couldn't wait
To see all their Twit faces!)

And off, with a smirk, that naughty Frynch crept,
To the place where he knew all those silly Twits slept.

Then he slithered and slunk, with a smile like a snadget,
Around the whole town, and he took every gadget!

He took all their mobiles, he took the PCs,
He took all the internet-ready TVs.

He took the computers, he took the laptops,
He took the iPhones, the iPads and iPlops.

And when he had grabbed all the items above,
He started to take other things the Twits love,
He took all their LOLs and their LMAOs,
He stole their hash tags from their little hash toes.

He snatched their Retweets and their mentions and then
He snaffled the Trending Topics Top Ten.
He kidnapped their followers, erased their DMs.
They all went in his sack, which he threw in the Thames.

Then he sat on the bank and he nervously waited,
With his lip fully bit and his breath fully bated
Until the sun rose. But then the Frynch frowned,
'They're just waking up . . . but what is that strange sound?'

All the Twits down in Twitville, the princes and bums
Were talking – without a device near their thumbs!
They chatted, they laughed, they guffawed and they chortled,
They sang and they shouted, they sniffed and they snortled.

The butchers, the bakers, the students and tourists,
The housewives, the bankers, the fish pedicurists,
The teachers, the stalkers, the geeks and the druids,
They actually met and swapped bodily fluids!

And the Frynch heard this sound, this unheard-of kerfuffle,
And he frowned and he blinked and he started to snuffle.

He HADN'T stopped Twitmas from coming!
It CAME!
Somehow or other, it came just the same!

The Frynch groped for hours, 'till his dongle was sore.
Then the Frynch thought of something he hadn't before!
'Maybe Twitter,' he thought, 'doesn't come from a phone.
'Maybe Twitter … perhaps … has a life of its own?'

And what happened then … ?
Well, in court they did say
That the Frynch's small dongle
Grew three sizes that day!

And the minute his dongle had started to swell,
He looked at the gadgets and cried 'Bloody Hell,
What a silly old git!' and he fell to the floor,
'What a nitwit-tit-git I have been, that's for sure!'

And ashamed and aroused, he went back to the town,
Dongle proudly erect but his head hanging down.
'I'm sorry,' he said, 'But could you, at a pinch,
Bear to forgive me, this silly old Frynch?'

And the Twits took one look at this figure forlorn,
With his chin on his chest and his confidence torn,
'Well, it's true' they replied, 'that we do need some closure.'
So they jailed him for theft and indecent exposure.

The Day After the Night Before Christmas

So the big day has arrived at last and once the presents have been opened, played with and broken, the highlight is The Christmas Dinner – that special once-a-year time when the whole family can put its problems to one side and gather together to pull crackers, wear silly hats and enjoy a hearty home-made feast.

My family's favourite is my legendary Twelve Days of Christmas Dinner but sadly, in these credit crunch times it can be awfully difficult to get hold of 12 drummers drumming, 11 pipers piping, 10 lords a-leaping, 9 ladies dancing, 8 maids a-milking, 7 swans a-swimming, 6 geese a-laying, 5 gold rings, 4 colly birds, 3 French hens and 2 turtle doves, let alone a partridge in a pear tree to stuff them in, so instead, here's my slightly more economical alternative. Not only delicious but also a real time- and washing-up-saver.

EDNA'S ALL-IN-ONE CHRISTMAS DINNER

INGREDIENTS:

One large turkey (giblets and packaging removed)

Spam (maple cured or oak smoked)

Brussels sprout, one

Can of barley wine

Bottle of sherry, one or more

Mince pie, one

Other miscellaneous ingredients

PREPARATION TIME: Six years, approximately.

METHOD:

Christmas Day can be a very stressful occasion, but I always find that preparing dinner helps me to relax. First, place the turkey in a deep baking tray filled with salt water and gin. Leave to soak overnight. Refill every two hours to compensate for what Stephen calls 'perfectly normal alcohol evaporation and nothing suspicious whatsoever'.

On Christmas morning, place turkey in tray on waist-high kitchen surface and proceed to 'tease' the skin. This involves puckering up and loosening the turkey skin from the carcass. To help you with this process, imagine you are gently massaging your husband's scalp. When the skin is completely loose, carefully place the slices of wafer-thin cured Spam under the skin. This will help moisten the turkey during cooking, while giving it that unmistakeable Spammy flavour.

Gently pat down the skin. Again, imagine you are massaging your husband's scalp (as if you haven't got enough to do already, while he just sits there munching Quality Street and fiddling with his trouser area). Slowly increase the pressure and frequency (as he flicks endlessly from channel to channel trying to find the darts, like the big lazy lump he is). If you find that pummelling the bird relentlessly with your fists isn't sufficient, try using a rolling pin. Or throw crockery at it.

When you reach this point, place the husband, I mean turkey to one side, take the can of barley wine and pour down your throat.

Next, take the Brussels sprout and the mince pie. Carefully lift the pastry lid of the pie, place the sprout underneath and replace lid. You may need to remove some of the filling to make room but never fear – waste not, want not – this can be used to help stick down the wrapping paper on those last minute gifts!

Next comes the all-important Christmas pudding. To ensure that all the flavours are at their peak, this needs to be made several years in advance and stored in a cold, airtight storage area – I generally use the children's bedroom. Make a small indentation in the top of the pudding with your little finger. It may help to imagine you are playfully sticking your finger in your husband's ear. Keep pressing until you feel a soft, squidgy substance. Then remove your finger and push the mince and sprout pie in as far as it will go. You will find this an intensely satisfying and calming experience.

The next stage can be a little messy so I would advise you to wear rubber gloves. I would also advise against imagining any part of your husband's anatomy at this point. Pull open the turkey's legs as wide as you can, then close your eyes and stuff your pudding deep and hard into the waiting crevice. Once this has been done, place the bird into your oven at the right temperature (this will vary depending on the size of the bird and your family's immune system). Then take the bottle of sherry, go and lie on your bed and sleep until Boxing Day.

CHRISTMAS ENTERTAINMENT

Once Christmas dinner is over and the family is well and truly stuffed, there's nothing nicer than a bit of entertainment to aid the digestive system. This is one of the easiest parts of Christmas Day. Simply take the trays off your laps and turn the volume up on the television. For those without a TV guide, here's a selection of some of the finest family favourites for your festive viewing this, and every other, year.

The Silence of the Reindeer – Anthony Hopkins is crazy old Kriss 'the Killer' Kringle, whose annual serial-murder spree is jeopardised when his bungling nephew, played by Will Ferrell, takes over one crazy Christmas Eve. Memorable for the classic lines 'Can you help me get this sofa onto the back of my sleigh?' and 'I ate his liver with a mince pie and a nice glass of sherry'.

You Ain't Half Hot, Mum – a special festive edition of the classic Seventies sitcom about a middle-aged man still living with his mother. Mrs Rex's hopes for a fun family Christmas are scuppered when her son Oedipus wins a romantic mini-break to Clacton in the office raffle. Things get complex and it's laughs all the way as she attempts to spurn his madcap, inappropriate advances in a variety of hilarious ways!

The Snowman 2 – in this sequel to the much-loved animated tale set 30 years after the original, the little boy, still traumatised by the whole experience, has grown up to wander the streets of London in his pyjamas and dressing gown, talking to snowmen and trying unsuccessfully to fly. Features the haunting new Aled Jones song *I'm Walking In the Area*.

THE YEAR AFTER CHRISTMAS

Once the big day is over, there's just Boxing Day, the returning of gifts, the sales, assorted additional get-togethers, New Year's Eve and the hangovers to get through before life returns to its normal, predictable, dreary, uneventful state. Roll on, January, dears!

VALENTINE'S DAY

Valentine's Day is the most romantic day of the year – a day of love, passion and overpriced roses. Unless you're married, of course. Then it's pretty much the same as every other day. To be fair to Stephen, he does occasionally remember – often around April – and when he does I know I'll be made to feel like the most beautiful woman on earth. He'll dim the lights, open a bottle of Asti Spumante and make me wear his Angelina Jolie mask.

Being married needn't mean the end of romance, however. If you are prepared to make the effort, you will find that Valentine's Day can be every bit as exciting as it was when you were a love-sick teenager. You could book a table in a nice restaurant or take the day off work and whisk your partner off to Paris or Camber Sands. Personally, I like to use my culinary skills to create the perfect romantic evening.

Last year, I arranged for someone to baby-sit our children. She was a lovely old lady who lived on the next street – ever so sweet and a little absent-minded, so it was relatively easy to persuade her that she'd agreed to take care of them for the night. It's such a shame she's no longer with us, as we're constantly looking for a good babysitter, but she did survive until well past midnight which is better than average.

With the children out of the way and Stephen down the pub, I set about transforming our humble two-up two-down into a palace of romance. I drew the curtains, draped Stephen's red 'Keep Korma and Curry On' beer towel over the lampshade, popped his Barry White LP on the hi-fi and made for the kitchen to prepare my special romantic meal, St Valentine's Day Moussaka – a mouth-watering combination of lamb, aubergines, herbs, spices and chocolate mousse. I'll leave the rest to your imagination, dears – suffice to say, there wasn't much Ceefax watched *that* night . . .

HALLOWE'EN

Stephen's favourite holiday is undoubtedly Hallowe'en. He loves the fantasy, the mythology and the fact that he doesn't have to wear anything special. Very often, we'll spend the entire night watching back-to-back horror movies, starting with something slightly scary such as the original *Frankenstein* or *Alvin and the Chipmunks* before building up to stronger fare like *The Exorcist* and *The Texas Chainsaw Massacre* and ending with our wedding video.

As well as our horrorthon, we sometimes host our own Hallowe'en party. It's a wonderful opportunity to see old friends wearing ludicrous costumes, although some make more effort than others. Stephen usually just puts a pillowcase over his head. He can't even be bothered to cut out eyeholes.

He just spends the evening bumping into things and falling over, so he doesn't even bother to behave any differently than usual, either.

If, unlike Stephen, you want to make a bit of effort, you can make your own costume or hire one from a fancy dress shop – here's a list of the most popular Hallowe'en costumes, rated from one to ten in order of scariness.

---

1. Ghost
2. Witch
3. Vampire
4. Werewolf
5. Frankenstein
6. Frankenstein's monster
7. The Duracell Bunny (well, it scares Stephen)
8. Flying Monkey
9. Piers Morgan
10. Flying Piers Morgan

A traditional game played on Hallowe'en is Bobbing for Apples, in which children attempt to remove floating apples from a bowl of water using only their teeth. Ever inventive, our children have developed their own version – Appling for Bobs, in which they compete to see who can make the most money from selling items they've stolen from the local Apple store to either Bob the Fence or Bob the Nearly-new Computer Store manager.

EASTER

This is one of Stephen's favourite holidays – he just loves dressing up and hopping round the house and at Easter this behaviour is far less conspicuous. Over the years he's tried a number of different costumes but for me, his most effective was Glenn Close – I can still see the children's faces when he showed them what he'd done with the Easter Bunny.

CHAPTER NINE

A Problem Shared

E VEN the most successful marriage can encounter the occasional hurdle. Most are riddled with them. In this final chapter, I take a look at some of the most common marital problems and advise you how best to overcome or ignore them.

COMFORT

One of the greatest dangers in a relationship is that a couple simply becomes too comfortable with one another. This may sound like a positive thing but it can mean the death knell for a marriage. Familiarity breeds contempt, as they say. After a period of time (about a week in our case) a husband or wife might find themselves having to listen to their partner burping loudly and breaking wind. While in our marriage this was marginally preferable to having to listen to Stephen talk, it was nevertheless a concern.

So, what should you do if you and your spouse are becoming too comfortable together? One solution is to try to recapture that initial frisson of unfamiliarity, that time when you don't really know your partner terribly well and you are still trying to impress them. There are a number of ways this could be achieved – one or both of you could try wearing a new scent or artificial moustache, one or both of you could change your name by deed poll or one or both of you could take part in a witness protection programme. Each of these will introduce a much-needed element of uncertainty to your relationship and before you know it, you're closing the door when you go to the toilet and hiding text messages from your lover all over again.

SNORING

While an apparently harmless activity, snoring can be the bane of the married person's life – it can cause sleeplessness, exhaustion, irritability and an irrational (or rational) desire to murder your partner. If this is the case, I have the answer, dears. Scientists have now developed a special pillow which is 100% effective in stopping snoring – provided you hold it firmly enough.

THE REMOTE

Although, no doubt, a wonderful technological innovation, the television remote control is nevertheless the curse of the modern marriage. In days gone by, it was necessary to get up from the sofa, walk across the room and press a button or turn a dial on the television set in order to change the channel. Fortunately, there were only a couple of channels, otherwise it would have been necessary to change the living room carpet every few months. However, with the development of infra-red technology came the remote and with it a host of new channels, leading to a significant increase in marital conflict and having to change the sofa every few months.

Remote control envy, as relationship experts call it, can be highly destructive. Some wives – for it is almost always the husband who is guilty of dominating possession of the remote – go to great lengths to try to escape what they term 'flicking hell'. They hide the remote, remove the batteries and even throw it in the bin but all to no avail – I know from personal experience. While Stephen couldn't find a matching pair of socks or clean pair of underpants if they were right under his nose, he's like a bloodhound when it comes to finding his way home in a state of acute inebriation and locating the television remote. If you suffer from this seemingly insoluble situation, I have just one word of advice for you – divorce. It may seem drastic but it's really far more acceptable than the alternative – getting rid of the TV.

COMMUNICATION

Most couples will tell you the secret to a successful marriage is communication and I am in complete agreement. If you want to maintain matrimonial harmony, it's vital you keep communication to a bare minimum. My motto is 'If you don't talk, you can't argue'. Keep all exchanges as brief and to the point as possible and, whatever you do, never discuss your feelings. These are strictly for your diary or turning into angst-ridden poetry, not for airing in public or private. No good ever came from sharing your thoughts and dreams with your partner. A couple can be carrying on perfectly well when, completely out of the blue, one partner might happen to mention that he doesn't really like cheese or that he's always wanted to be a train driver. Or a woman. Revelations like these can only cause harm to a relationship and are far better kept to yourself. Of course, Stephen and I have no such secrets but we nevertheless keep all conversation as succinct and superficial as possible, often spending weeks avoiding each other entirely, just in case.

POLITICS AND RELIGION

On balance, I would say it's best to avoid discussions on religion in a marriage, unless one of you is the Pope. Theological matters have been a cause of great division and bloodshed throughout the centuries and, in my experience, there's quite enough of that in a marriage already, thank you very much.

Likewise, politics can be very disruptive as it can throw into sharp relief a couple's differing ideologies. Personally, I always say who I vote for is a matter between me and the ballot box, as is my recipe for Spam Bourguignon and where I keep my premium bond winnings.

SCIENCE

One of the many curses of the modern marriage is DNA testing. While it can be a highly effective and entertaining plot device on *CSI Miami* and *Jeremy Kyle*, it can be a minefield for those of us living in the real world, causing no end of trauma. In fact, Stephen was so suspicious that he recently arranged for a paternity test of his own. I can still see the look of anguish on his face when it revealed that most of the children were his.

THE IN-LAWS

When you marry someone, you're not so much gaining a husband or wife as gaining a husband or wife and a husband or wife's parents, otherwise known, from that day forth, as the in-laws. In-laws can come in all shapes and sizes. They can be warm and welcoming or daunting and destructive. The relationship between a wife and her mother-in-law, for example, can be an extremely challenging one. There can be a huge amount of unexpected jealousy and resentment – there certainly was in our case. But eventually some kind of truce was established between us as I was forced to accept that, no matter what, Stephen was never going to go back to her.

INFIDELITY

Infidelity can invade the sanctity of even the most devoted marriage. While not as serious a problem as those I have covered up to this point, it can still be a cause of considerable tetchiness. If you suspect your partner may be having an affair, there are several tell-tale signs that can confirm it. These are different, depending whether the husband or wife is the adulterer.

The wife's demeanour may become distant and preoccupied. She could get a new hairstyle and suddenly start going out more, possibly to spend time with 'an old school friend'. You may find she becomes forgetful and neglects certain daily tasks such as checking the use-by date on the yoghurt and making the children's packed lunch. She may mope around the garden, humming the theme from *Love Story* and saying things like, 'Where do you think this marriage is heading?' and, 'Do you still love me?'.

The husband's demeanour may be erratic and bouncy. He could get a new pair of underpants and suddenly start going out more to spend time with 'that dancer with the tattoos from the Bongo-bongo Club'. You may find he becomes forgetful and neglects certain daily tasks such as placing three-horse accumulator bets at Chepstow and going down the pub. He may dance around the living room in his underpants, singing *Mr Lover-lover* and say things like 'Still got it' and 'Yippee-ki-yay'.

So, let's assume your spouse is having an affair – what should you do now? Personally, I'm in accordance with Tammy Wynette when she sings *Stand By Your Man*. At least, I would be if I could find his stand by button. The important thing is not to panic. Look on the positive side – an affair needn't be a bad thing. It could be the wake-up call you needed, reminding you that you have been neglecting your partner. It could also result in a huge amount of guilt and shame, meaning you might get that nice pair of shoes you've always wanted. At the very least, it will mean you've got the house to yourself a bit more often, so everyone's a winner! If it weren't for her at number 38, I don't know when I'd get time for my sudokus.

OTHER PROBLEMS

It's obviously impossible for me to address every single obstacle you are likely to encounter in your married life in one chapter. However, if I have missed your particular problem, don't worry, dear – just read on and, with any luck, you'll find the advice you so desperately need.

The other day, I was taking a long walk in the park when a young lady came up to me. Her eyes were red from crying and her hand shook as she took hold of my arm and said quietly, 'Mrs Fry, I have a terrible, personal problem. You're so very kind and wise. Could you please give me some advice?'

I looked deep into her teary eyes. How could I possibly ignore this poor woman's words? I knew exactly what to do – I went straight home and rang the local evening newspaper. They were terribly excited at the prospect of a local celebrity offering their services as an Agony Aunt – or Agony Cousin as I insisted on being referred to (the term Aunt implies a woman of a certain age and my age has always been extremely uncertain – particularly to Stephen). I knew it was my duty to use my kindness and wisdom to help all those poor, desperate souls out there. The *Local Evening Gazette* has kindly allowed me to reproduce my very first column, covering the topics of food and relationships, in this book. Unfortunately, the incompetent editor of the newspaper somehow contrived to place my answers to the relationships questions in the food section and vice versa. However, it still caused quite a stir, by all accounts.

DEAR EDNA...

Food

Dear Edna,
What's the secret to cooking a really great Sunday lunch?

It's all about instinct, dear. Some people put their heart and soul into it. Others prefer to take their time and savour every moment of the process. Personally, I like to close my eyes until it's finished.

Dear Edna,
I love spaghetti bolognese but I can't chop an onion without crying. Do you have any tips?

I have a similar problem, dear. I find that smearing it

liberally with I Can't Believe It's Not Butter generally does the trick. Alternatively, you could leave it out altogether.

Dear Edna,
I'm entering this year's W.I. pancake making competition but mine are always so limp and tasteless. How can I make the perfect pancake?

You can find all sorts of helpful 'ingredients' online these days, dear. Failing that, there's always Nigella.

Dear Edna,
How do you know when Stephen's sausage is done?

He sings *God Save the Queen* and falls asleep.

Dear Edna,
You're such a culinary marvel. What dishes do you enjoy cooking the most?

Anything as long as it's quick and relatively painless, dear.

Dear Edna,
Where do you get all the ingredients for your wonderful meals?

Lidl, the Co-op and the bins round the back of Sainsbury's.

Relationships

Dear Edna,

I'm 25 and still a virgin. I've just started a relationship with an older, more experienced man and I don't want to disappoint him. What should I do?

First, make sure you have a full range of utensils and a good, sturdy kitchen table. Clean up as you go along and whatever you do, don't leave it in too long. Then, it's on with the rubber gloves ...

Dear Edna,

My boyfriend is a bit on the large side. What should I do?

If it makes your eyes water, you could try biting on a spoon. Or perhaps do it underwater?

Dear Edna,

My husband is having erectile problems. Could you recommend anything?

If it looks a bit limp, make sure you have a firm grip then toss as hard as you can. If it still doesn't look good enough to win a prize, just add a little lemon juice and you should have something all the ladies will be happy to stick in their mouths.

Dear Edna,
How can you be sure Stephen is completely satisfied?

I always prick it with a fork until the juices run clear.

Dear Edna,
I'm worried our lovemaking is becoming repetitive. What sexual positions would you suggest to liven things up?

There's the Toad in the Hole, The Triple Decker Pork Sandwich and, if I'm feeling particularly adventurous, the Pineapple Surprise.

Dear Edna,
Where do you fantasise about making love?

Lidl, the Co-op and the bins round the back of Sainsbury's.

Of course, if a problem shared is a problem halved then a problem shared with thousands must be so small you could barely see it with a microscope. So the moment my loyal readers discovered I was writing a book about marriage, they bombarded me with all manner of marital questions, some of which I present here for your amusement, together with the names of those seeking my advice, as I feel that public humiliation is a crucial part of any personal improvement process.

Dear Edna,

What do you do when your partner asks you to cut their toenails for them?

Andrew

Personally, I go to the launderette. Believe me, dear, this is only the tip of the iceberg – it starts with toenails but before you know it, it's eyebrow-trims, scalp massages and actually listening to them when they tell you about their day. If your partner is unwilling to cut their own toenails, I suggest you direct them to a branch of Piranha Pedicures – one visit and I guarantee neither you nor they will have to worry about their toenails again.

Dearest Edna,

My wife Marie currently lives in New York City and, with me here in England, I often find that the vast distance tends to put our relationship under some strain. An extra-marital affair seems like an awful lot of hard work for very little reward, but can you perhaps suggest some ways we can keep our marriage alive whilst she is so far away and, undoubtedly I am sure, having a great deal more fun than I am?

Yours in genial frustration,

Rory

You really shouldn't fret, Rory dear. I haven't visited New York myself but I can't imagine it has any more to offer than your own home town. I'm sure it doesn't have any more restaurants, theatres, museums or skyscrapers and I'd be surprised if there were any kind of public park where your dear wife could frolic shamelessly on the grass with a string of swarthy, muscular Italian Adonises.

Instead of getting yourself into a state, I recommend that you relieve your frustration by joining a gymnasium or sports club. Failing that, a systematic programme of self-abuse and regular bouts of gentle sobbing should do the trick.

Dear Edna,

My wife and I have always approached the issue of changing nappies on the basis that whoever first notices the event deals with it. A combination of teething and solid food intake on the part of our youngest child has resulted in occasional nappies of extraordinary and eye-watering pungency, but my wife has never yet been the one to change them. As much as I love and trust my wife, I have come to the conclusion that she is deliberately ignoring the "wind of change" to avoid the consequences. What can I do to redress the balance without neglecting the child in question?

Tom

Hello Tom dear,

As the wife of a serial non-nappy changer and mother of numerous noxious children, you have my deepest sympathy. I had hoped that over the years the situation would improve but, if anything, since the birth of our latest (and hopefully last) child, things have got even worse. From the moment the breastfeeding ended and he was moved onto solids, he simply refused to have anything to do with the baby.

However, I'm quite sure that, being a woman, your wife is not deliberately ignoring the situation. I expect she simply suffers from sinusitis or some other nasally-challenging condition. I recommend a decongestant such as a tablet or nasal spray and before you know it, you'll both be sharing in the beautiful miracle that is your own child's excrement.

Dear Edna,

One of my friends is working on his second divorce, i.e. he's about to remarry. I've strongly advised him to sign a pre-nup this time. Prenuptial agreements, in my humble view, are essential to having an Almost Perfect Marriage. If only because it ensures you're both in it for the right reasons. Having your heart broken is bad enough, but it's worse when you haven't planned to protect your assets. My friend says it's awfully unromantic to be keeping an eye on the exit as one walks down the aisle. To pre-nup or not to pre-nup, what's your view? Any wise words for my friend?

Rieke

If it's wise words you're looking for, you couldn't have come to a better place, dear – wisdom is one of my middle names, together with wit, beauty and Bathsheba. Prenuptial agreements are a notoriously tricky area, as I have touched on earlier in the book although in my view, anything that diminishes the romance of your wedding day is probably a good thing. Otherwise you and your partner will have unrealistic expectations of your marriage. Far better to make a clear, legally-binding public commitment to your future separation.

Sadly, when I married Stephen I was young-ish and foolish. I believed our love would last forever – or at least, longer than three days. If only we had signed a pre-nuptial agreement, who knows where I would be now ...?

... So sorry, dear, I lost my train of thought for a moment. As far as your 'friend' is concerned, I would suggest doing a little research before bringing the subject up – I understand there is quite a boom in Prenuptial Agreement companies, many promising a considerable payout even if you have no intention of getting married.

Dear Edna,

By all accounts your marriage is as near to perfect as one could hope for, but surely there must be days, as you spiral further and further into the background of Stephen's ever-expanding lime-light, where you've simply had enough and you want to run, screaming like a banshee, into the hills and never return? How do you handle these emotions, keep up your sense of self worth, hang on to your individuality and continue to portray your cheery demeanour?

Lindy

You appear to have been misinformed, Lindy dear – if anyone is in danger of spiralling further and further into the background, it is my husband and not myself. He may have something that is forever expanding but it certainly isn't his limelight, dear. No doubt, you have been misled by his Twitter output like so many others – I'm afraid his tweets are little more than the imaginings of a man floundering in his wife's considerable shadow. I try to reassure him that my new-found fame doesn't make him any less of a man – I tell him time and time again that that simply isn't possible – but, for some reason, he still feels the need to subject the online community to his fevered ramblings.

As for running, screaming like a banshee, never to return, I have to say that, if anything, my scream is more akin to a chiming bell although the rest sounds distinctly appealing. And my cheery demeanour, as you so delightfully put it, is the result of years of practice in front of the bathroom mirror. And the occasional gin.

Dear Edna,

I am a firm believer in looking my best for my husband every day (hair, make-up, tortuous underwear and so forth) but he is happy to wander about looking like a delegate at a rough sleepers' convention. All our friends tease him about it but he just doesn't give a monkey's. What should I do?

Fiona

I sympathise completely with your plight, dear. Like you, I see it as a woman's role to look her very best for her husband - or at least, any man who might turn up unexpectedly when he's out. I am scrupulous about the way I look and never get out of bed without full make-up and my very best hat.

Sadly, my current husband shares the same disregard for his appearance as your own. I can't tell you how many times he's arrived at a respectable social function without a tie. Or jacket. Or trousers. Of course, I've tried to change him – literally – as it is every wife's duty to do, but to no avail. I've lost count of the times I've taken him to the Arndale centre to get a new set of clothes but he only wanders off and gets lost. I've even tried burning his existing assortment but he only noticed when the bar staff at the King's Head refused to serve him unless he covered his you-know-what with the wine menu (not an easy task as they only do house red and white).

I'm afraid to say that, at the end of the day, all you can do, dear, is ignore him. In public, at least. Sooner or later he'll get the message – and if he doesn't, just try to remember why you married him in the first place. That's right, dear – fear of growing old alone in a house full of cats and collectable thimbles.

Dear Edna,

*My partner and I have been together for a little over 7 years …
our 7-year itch has still not arrived. We are wondering what we
could be doing wrong. Please help us – what did you and Stephen*

*do to progress the arrival of your 7-year itch and how long did
it last?*

   Thanking you,
   Ruth

Hello Ruth dear,

Don't worry – no matter how secure you think your
relationship is, there will inevitably come a time when
one or the other of you will find your eye wandering and
before you know it you're having an affair with your optician. Relationship experts call this the 'seven-year itch'
because, apparently, that's the length of time into a marriage that infidelity is most likely to occur. I have to admit
that I find this a slightly depressing statistic as with Stephen it happened after three days (it would have been less
but it took him that long to find his way out of the wedding cake).

Personally, I think it's best to get it over with as quickly
as possible then you can both get on with your various
infidelities at your own pace. To facilitate this, I would
suggest you take things into your own hands – or someone else's hands to be more accurate. Introduce him to
any attractive friends, if you have any. If not, a work col-
league would do equally well. In extreme circumstances
– if, for example, he's repellent to other women – you
could consider employing the services of a professional
you-know-what worker. If you do, be sure to choose one
from the top of the range or half-way up, at least. You will
find that their English is more fluent and they will be
more discreet and have their own towel.

Dear Edna,

My husband is a plane spotter and it is starting to take over our lives. I don't mind the collection of model planes he keeps in his den or the stash of aircraft magazines I found under the bed, I've come to enjoy our regular holidays under the Heathrow flight path, and I have even got used to the runway he has built in the garden (the conversion of the shed into a control tower was quite a feat!), but now he wants us to sell the house and move into a converted 747. I wouldn't be surprised if he asks me to dress up as an air hostess and serve all his meals on a trolley. What should I do?

Heather Culpin

Personally, I would go for the British Airways uniform, Heather dear – the stitching is more reliable and the skirt allows greater freedom of movement than other low-cost airlines. As for the trolley, make sure it has a heated compartment to ensure his meals are kept nice and warm and is made of a strong but pliant material – crucial should you experience excessive turbulence.

As for the rest of it, dear, I really wouldn't distress yourself if I were you – you should see the magazines Stephen keeps under the bed. And in the airing cupboard. And on top of the cistern. I never know when I'm going to come across another one – if it weren't for all the bodybuilding ones, I'd worry he that I was living with some kind of you-know-what maniac! And as for living in an aeroplane, I wouldn't be too concerned, if I were you. I'm quite sure he doesn't really intend to do any such thing – you know what men are like. He's probably just trying to persuade you to leave him.

Dear Edna,

My great passion is travel. I adore going somewhere unfamiliar and exploring foreign places, and would dearly love to take an overseas holiday with my other half. He, however, is not so inclined. He says travel doesn't interest him and that he's never had a hint of wanderlust. He also has a fear of flying, and although a long flight could be made quite comfortable for him through the use of drugs, alcohol and business class, he remains unmoveable. How can I persuade him otherwise, and convince him of the wonderful experiences that await us if we look further afield than places we can merely drive to?

Samantha Russell

Hello Samantha dear,

You should count yourself lucky – Stephen starts to panic if he spends more than an hour away from the sofa. Even when he goes to the Dog & Duck, he needs several Bacardi Breezers before he can really relax. We have managed the occasional family trip, even abroad, but I generally have to sedate him first due to his fear of flying, fear of sailing, fear of hovercrafts and fear of anything foreign (except lagers, strangely). Of course, once he's actually there he has a lovely time even if he refuses to admit it. He's the only person I know who can sulk while drinking shots off the runner-up in a poolside Miss Wet T-shirt competition.

If drugging or kidnapping is out of the question, why not try something more subtle such as tampering with the satnav? Before he knows it, he'll be at the airport and his fait will be at least half accompli. Then all you'll have to negotiate is his blind terror at the thought of being thousands of feet in the air in a giant metal tube. On the odd occasion that Stephen has accidentally regained consciousness before passing through the customs gate, I find that a calming hand on the shoulder and a few well-chosen words do wonders. I've always found the phrases 'Stop being such a big girl's blouse' and 'Duty free' to be particularly effective.

If, however, none of the above proves successful and your wanderlust is undiminished, you have two choices. The first is to travel alone. I have done this a few times myself but I can't honestly say I would recommend it. No matter how far you travel, no matter what sights you see, what delicacies you eat and what fascinating people you meet, you still have to return home to find your husband's still there. The second is to swap husbands with Heather. I'm quite sure she would be amenable – he sounds like a dreadful man.

EDNA'S FOOLPROOF
INSTANT MARITAL RESCUER

If, after reading my advice to those poor unfortunate people, you still feel concerned, there's no need, thanks to my Foolproof Instant Marriage Rescuer. No matter what you believe is at the heart of your marital discord, I assure you, you are merely scratching the surface. In order to truly work out your differences, you need to go a little deeper. Simply fill in the two following sections as completely as possible, leaving no stone unturned and no wound un-reopened. Be as wide-ranging and brutally honest as possible and you will then have the basis for a discussion which I believe will have a significant and irrevocable effect on your marriage.

MY FAULTS

MY PARTNER'S FAULTS

MY PARTNER'S FAULTS

MY PARTNER'S FAULTS

MY PARTNER'S FAULTS

DIVORCE

If, after completing the previous task, you feel that an Almost Perfect Marriage is simply an aspiration too far for you and your partner, you're probably right. In truth, very few couples ever experience the kind of marriage Stephen and I share – the important thing is that you bought this book before you came to that conclusion. If you are one (or two) of these people, then you needn't be concerned as there is a perfectly satisfactory alternative – divorce. Some couples opt for mere separation but, to my mind, this demonstrates a lack of commitment.

However, if you're still not quite sure whether you have the strength to make that final break, then I have one last piece of advice for you. I would suggest that the problem might be all inside your head, dear. You see, the answer is terribly easy if you take it logically. I'd really like to help you in your struggle to be free. By my reckoning, there must be 50 ways to leave your husband . . .

> Just hop on a plane, Jane,
> Push him under a tram, Pam,
> Make him watch *Sex and The City 2*, Sue,
> Just get yourself free.

> Say you're really a man, Jan,
> Hold a pillow over his face, Grace,
> Stop shaving your legs, Megs
> And set yourself free.

Now, it's really not my habit to butt in. And, as you know dear, I've no desire to make your cranium spin, so just sit quietly while I pour another gin and tell you about those 50 ways to leave your husband ...

> Buy him low alcohol beer, Rhia,
> Knit him a sweater, Loretta,
> Tell him he's not as good in bed as your ex, Becks
> Just get yourself free.

> Find a new fella, Stella,
> Focus on your career, Maria,
> Refuse to do it on the kitchen table, Mabel
> And give him the big E.

You know, dear, it grieves me so to see you in such pain. I'll pour that Spam Masala safely down the drain while I endeavour further to explain about those 50 ways to leave your husband ...

> Just pack all your bags, Mags,
> Bore him to death, Beth,
> Tell him the truth, Ruth
> There's no need to shout.

> Tell him you're pregnant again, Gwen,
> Spoil Match of the Day, Faye,
> Stick his hand in the blender, Brenda
> And get yourself out.

Now, I suggest you get a good night's sleep, dear, and in the morning everything will be quite clear. But if not, just have another glass of beer. After all, there must be 50 ways to leave your husband …

> Find a toyboy, Joy,
> Get a ticket to Scarborough, Barbara,
> Say you'll do anything for love but you won't do that, Pat,
> And start a new life

> Put his porn in the bin, Lynn,
> Change the locks while he's at a Monster Truck Rally, Sally,
> Let him walk in on you with the man from the garden centre
>   on ya, Tonya,
> And stop being his wife

Well, I do hope that helps you with the task you have at hand, and you'll have no trouble removing that golden band. I apologise that my poem rarely scanned. And that there were only 24 ways to leave your husband.

In Conclusion ...

MARRIAGE ISN'T A BOWL OF CHERRIES. IT isn't all drinking pina coladas and getting caught in the rain. Marriage is joy and sadness, pleasure and pain. And more pain and more sadness. Marriage is that look of love in your husband's eyes when he arrives home at three in the morning, accompanied by the local constabulary and a monkey. Marriage is sharing a private joke together at your children's expense. Marriage is swings and roundabouts, see-saws and slides, cider bottles and syringes. Marriage is watching your husband while he sleeps, and him watching other women while they sleep. Marriage is chaos and calm, laughter and tears, bangers and cream and strawberries and mash. It's give and take, hide and seek and hit and run. But above all, marriage is about wanting to share your life with someone you really, truly love but staying with your spouse instead, no matter how much they irritate and ignore you.

Hopefully now, after reading this book, you'll know exactly what it means to have an Almost Perfect Marriage and, despite all the statistics, you'll be much closer to having an Almost Perfect Marriage of your own. It has been an absolute delight to share my marital experiences with you. I hope it has been a help to you – I know I feel much better now, thank you.

My sincere love and sympathy,
Edna Fry (Mrs)

Index

P UBLISHER'S NOTE – Owing to tight publication deadlines, there was insufficient time to assign page numbers to the following subjects or to place them in strict alphabetical order. We hope this doesn't affect your enjoyment of this index.

D

David Dimbleby

E

Elephantine
Edible undergarments
Eternal youth – the secret of
Emissions – carbon, nocturnal
Enhancement – surgical
Even strokes
Exes – a guide including artex,
    latex, spandex
Excessive seepage and how to
    staunch it

F

Friction
Full-frontal photographs
Flanelling
Fundamentally wrong,
    even in Thailand
Fumbling
Funnel grunting – definition and
    diagram
Fig rolls
Feather dusters

G

G-spot – exact location
Girth

H

Habits – disgusting, nuns',
    disgusting nuns'
How to keep your man completely

satisfied
How to keep your woman
    completely satisfied
How to keep your next-door
    neighbour completely satisfied
Hostess trolleys – uses and abuses

I

Inappropriate nuzzling
Inappropriate nozzling
Inflatable – castles, dolls,
    Dannii Minogue
In-bred
In bread
In-laws – getting on with,
    getting off with
Insertion
Illegal,
    even in Amsterdam

J

Jaw-dropping pictures

K

Kettling – where to insert
    the spout
Kinky or quirky?

L

Lottery – how to win it every
    week. A foolproof system.
Libido
Ludo
Livestock
Living room

dancers
Three – course dinner, piece suite,
    somes
Treacle
Tickling
Trickling (*see* treacle)
Tugging too hard

U

Unexpected guests
Unexpected gusts
Unacceptable behaviour
Under no circumstances is that
    thing coming anywhere near
    me tonight
Unsightly blemishes
Una Stubbs

V

Vaseline
Vibrations – good, bad, ugly
Vaguely familiar – acquaintances,
    family members

W

Water – works, proofs, bed,
    boarding
Weapon – concealed, congealed,
    using you-know-what as a
Wedded bliss and how to
    guarantee it
Wet room
Wriggle room
Wrong on so many levels

X

Xeroxing – divorce papers,
genitalia
XL, L, M or S? The importance of
    size, particularly when xeroxing

Z

Zebra crossings and other
    dangerous places to do
    you-know-what
Zookeepers' uniforms

Y

Yodelling at the crucial moment
Yawning at the crucial moment
Y-fronts

Subscribers

UNBOUND is a new kind of publishing house. Our books are funded directly by readers. This was a very popular idea during the late eighteenth and early nineteenth century. Now we have revived it for the Internet age. It allows authors to write the books they really want to write and readers to support the writing they would most like to see published.

The names listed below are of readers who pledged their support and made this book happen. If you'd like to join them, visit: www.unbound.co.uk.

Richard & Lisa Abdy
Thomas Abert
Maria Adamiak
Carolyn Adams
Rachelle Adams
Dawn Adams
Jessica Coover
Adelman
Bethany Adlam
David Adler
Roel Adriaans

Joris Aerts
Sasha Afanasieva
Erik Agterberg
Laura Ahern
Malachi Aird
Mireille Albeda-
   Riesenbeck
Wyndham Albery
Chris Allan
Isabelle Allison
Malaika Allsopp

Ursula Altmeyer
Scott Ambidge
Lynn Andrews
Terrie Anthony
Claire Archer
Agnes Ardiyanti
James Armstrong
Vanessa Armstrong
Fred Armstrong
Craig Arnush
Gail Ashington

Noel Aslett
Lucy Atkinson
Amy Au-Yong
Catherine Austin
Diana Austin
Heather Baier
Martin Bailey
Gemma Baimbridge
Karen Baines
Marian Baker
Sal Ball
Maria Raich Balp
Jane Bancroft
Victoria Banfield
Jasmine Banister
Courtney Barefoot
Hani Barghouthi
Jean Barkocy
Donna Barley
Julie & David Barlow
Leah Barr
Madeline Bassett
Amelia Bateman
Gareth Arend Batty
Albany Bautista
Marie Bayes
Emma Bayliss
Jacqueline Beard
Judy Becher
Thorhalla
    Gudmundsdottir
    Beck
Ceri Bedford
Emma Harrison
Beesley

Alice Beilby
Sarah Belgrove
Tim Bell
Rachel Bell
Jennifer Benge
Melissa Benjamin
Magne Bergland
Paul Berry
Megan Beveridge
Shuana Bharatia
Metal Bijou
Monica Binanti
Emma Bird
Debbie Bird
Janet Bishop
Carmel & Jason Black
Julie Blackburn
Debbie Blancharde
Tory Blyth
Els Boer
Karima Barnes &
    Simon Boice
Anna Maria Boland
Ron Bossley
Otley and Botley
Kate Bott
Stephen Boucher
Martijn Bouterse
Paul Bowley
Colin Bown
Steven Bown
J. Patience Boyd
Amy P. G. Brazelton
LTC Jon P. Brazelton
    US Army

Heather Briggs
Cathy Broaders
Sheena & Paul Brockett
Amanda Brogan
L. Withers & T. Brooke
Anthony Ryan &
    Simon Brookes
Alan Kenneth Brooks
Marcella Brown
Justin Browning-Smith
Phil Bruce-Moore
Maria Bueno
Matt Builth
Edwin Buising
Natalie Bunch
Nicola Burden
Fiona Burg
Michael Burn
Duncan & Claire-
    Louise Burns
Sarah Burrell
Debbie Burton
Ian Buxton
David Callier
Claire Cameron
Andrew Campbell
Sue Campbell
Helen Campbell-
    Woodrup
Alison Campling-
    Williams
Debbie Carnell
Sarah Carolan
Alex Carpenter
Larissa Carpenter

Alex Carr
Suzanne Carroll
Susan Carson
Sarah Carswell
Elizabeth Carter
Noel Carter
Nicola Carter
Anthony Casey
Langendries Catheline
Carol & Alan Causby
Jonathan Chaddock
Lisa Chadwick
Hilary Chaplin
Andy Chapman
Steve Chase
Mrs Cheese
Pietro Cheli
Joanna Chladek
George & Rachel
   Chopping
Jeanne & Chris
Charmian Christie
Stuart Christie
Sabrina Chung
Jonathan Churchman-
   Davies
Catherine Clapperton
Shelley Clark
Sarah Clarke
Laura Clarricoates
Karen Cleary
Linda Clinch
Nic Close
Gabi Coatsworth
Suzanne Cobb

David Cochrane
Martin Cohen
Lisa Cohn-
   Kroonenberg
Marianne Cole
David & Susan Cole
Chris Coleman
Vaughan Coleridge-
   Matthews
Catherine Colley
Jo Collimore
Catherine Collopy
Liz Conlan
Jacqueline Connell
Rob Cook
Kay Cook
Claire Coombes
Caroline Cooper
Jill Copping
Emma Corbett
Tom Corder
Christopher Corneschi
Linda Corrin
Elaine Cottrell
Carole Coutanche
Rachael Cox
Dawn Coxwell
Catherine Craddock
Ross Craig
Jane Crane
Sarah Crane
Beth Crisp
Sarah Crook
Kate Crossley
Amber Cuenca

Sue Cullen
Heather Culpin
Beris Cumming
Graham Cunningham
Hoke & Virginia Currie
Jennifer Curtis
Alex Cvitanovic
Veerle d'Haens
James Dakin
Lisa & Mark Dalton
Karin Dannberg
Steven Darby
Ruth Darling
Kerry Daud
Lissa Davenport
Jen Davies
Viv Davies
Claire Davies
Christine A. Davies
Brenda Kathleen Davies
Charlotte Daw
Belinda Daws
Michelle Day
Maria De Barros
Marianne de Kok
Rosanne de Nijs
Rachel De Rienzo
J. McPherson &
   A. de Totth
Michelle de Villiers
Sanne de Vries
Heleen de Vries
Julie Deal
Sarah Deane
Marjan Debevere

Stuart Deeley
John Devonport
John Dexter
Elizabeth Dhadwar
Louise Diamond
Arjen Dijkstra
Ben Dijkstra
Sarah Dilnot
Vivian Diodati
Sally Dobbins
Ruth Dockerty
Helen Domaracki
Karen Donnachie
Wendalynn Donnan
Bill Donnelly
Claire Dore
Natalie Dorey
Jan Dorsett
Emma Doward
Maggie Down
Chris Downs
Kat Downward
John Dredge
Karen Ducat
Maria Dunbar
Stephen Durbridge
Melissa Dwyer
Christine Dye
Laurence Eagle
Debra Eagle
Graham East
Giulio Ecchia
Tracey Eckert
Alison Edgson
Patrick Karlsson

Edlund
Katherine Edward
Andrew S. R. Edwards
Paul Edwards
Lisa Edwards
Ines Eggimann
John Ellams
Lynsey Ellard
Dave Kay &
    Nick Elliott
Stephanie Elliott
Trish Ellis
Frank Endrullat
Chris Enright
Lee Eskriett
Dr Mike Evans
Karen Evans
Allyson Evans
Katie Evans
Rose Evans
Harma Everts
Isobel Fairburn
Anna & Daniel
    Fairhead
Louise Farquharson
Shantelle Farrant-
    O'Brien
Gregory Fenby Taylor
Susannah Ferdinand
Faye Ferguson
Matt Fern
Adam & Fern Exmouth
Charles Fernyhough
Melissa Fine
Paul Fischer

Andi Fischer
Ian Fitzpatrick
Jackie Fitzpatrick
James Flavin
Siobhan Flesher
Alison Forbes
Sarah Forbes
Martin Ford
Ali Forrest
Debbie Foss
Aileen Foster
Tim Fothergill
Robert Fouldes
Ilana Fox
Debbie Fox
Christine Frankland
Mike Frankland
Emily Fraser
Robert Freeborn
Carl-Henrik
Salomonson Freij
John Frewin
Philip Fridd
Kelley Frizelle
Rosemarie Fullerton
Bob Fulton
Linzi Fung
Ian Furbank
Terry Furlong
Zoe G
Carrie Gabriel
Tanith Galer
Marie Gallagher
Kristine Garina
Alison Garner

Peta Garside
Jorge Garzon
Lucy Gaunt
Mr & Mrs Gaunt
Otley & Botley
Sonia Geissler
Hazel Gentle
Jasmine Georgin
Tony Gibbon
Amanda Gibbs
Simon Gibson
Gemma Gibson
Maggie Gilbert
Jane Goddard
Laura Goddard
Hayley Golding
P. Ricardo & S. Golding
Andrew Goldsmith
Jane Goodwin
Stuart Gornall
Vicki & Adrian
  Gostling
Randy Gouvas
Neil Graham
Neil Graham
Neil Graham
Sarah Gramelspacher
Alexandra Gray
Alison Gray
Dan Grayson
Amy Gregson
Emma Grimwood
Caroline Groocock
Helen Grout
Emma Guilbert

FireRose & Gumby
Anna Gustitus
Emily H
Kara Hahn
Patrick Hall
George Hall
Owen Hamnett
Jon & Laura Hanes
Kate Hanlon
Chris Hansen
Pete Harbord
Mike Hardcastle
Kate Hardcastle
Stewart Hardcastle
Elizabeth Harris
Christopher Harrison
Sue Hart
Katy Hart
Andy Hart
Jacqueline Hartnett
Jo Hartwell
Felicity Harvey
Dini Hashim
Georgina Havelock
Kaitlyn Hawking
Meg Hawkins
Sharon Hayes
Vikki Hayes
Patricia Healey
Jackie Healey
Samantha Heath
Martin Heavens
Tory Heazell
Sheila Heeps
Rose Dwight Heintz

Sara Held
Patricia Heldoorn
Emma Hendry
Leslie Henson
Phill Heselton
Krystel Rose Hewett
Glenda Hicks
Vicky Hill
Adi Himpson
Allison Hipkin
Joanna Hirst
Ren Hjorth
John & Maggie
  Hodgkiss
Emily Holden
Karen Ren Hollowell
  @kitschandquirky
Mairin Holmes
Teresa Honeywood
Petry Hoogenboom
Debbie Hooks
Cathy Hornby
Joanne How
Sian Howard
Erika Howard
Lorna Howarth
Sharon Howe-Jones
Julie Howells
Mark Hudson
Laura Hughes
Ella Humphreys
Jackie Humphreys
Andreas Husby
Lid Hutin
Linda Hutton

Thomas Huxley

John Hyatt

Sam Hyatt

Piet Ikbestaniet

Natalie Iles

Keith Ilyttmab

Flor deCanela &
   LlaBurra Ines

Sue Ireland

Ben & Izzy

Cathryn Jacob

Jacqueline James

Jean Jamieson

David Jamieson

Kimberley Jamieson

Haje Jan Kamps

Kayt Jarred

Kristie Jenkins

Paul Jenks

Jenny Jennings

Suzi Jobe

Rowena Johns

Laura Johnson

Gawain Jones

Christine Jones

Aimee Jones

Keith Jones

Deborah Jones-Davis

Clare Jordan

Elsje Jorritsma

Zoe Judd

Marie Juillard

Bilge Kaan Bölük

Richard Kang

Lisa Keane Elliott

Kalleedaneia <3

Kate Kellaway

Rachel Kelsey

Paula Kennedy

Heather Kennedy

Niall Nancy Kenny

Catherine Kent

Helen Kenyon

Audrey Keszek

Dan Kieran

Ann Kilby

Anne King

Emelie King

Elena King

Meg Kingston

Nicola Burdon Kirby

Jon & Victoria Kirk

Rebekah Kittl

Anna Kleshevnikova

Narell Klingberg

Ben Kock

Frank Kockelkoren

Marco Kok

Anna-Maria Kowalik

Hollie Kramer

Paul & Lars Kurth-
   Sugarsars

Fabrice Kutting

Michelle Ann Kwara

Leticia Lago

Peggy Langdown

Glenda Lau

Stephanie Willis Lawlor

Pamela Lawrence

Carolyn Lawson

Kim Le Patourel

Kay Batty Leahy

Jørgen Leditzig

Jonathan Lee

Justine Lee

Dylan Leeman

Leona Lees

Carol K. Leiren

Sara Letts

Michelle Leung

Wendy Lewis

Sue Lewis

Lucy Lewis

Katherine Lewton

Bart Libert

Claire Lickman

Mark Lilley

Camille Fong Lim

Jerrick Lim

Laura Lindsay

Liane Linstead

Robert Lister

David Lister

Douglas Livingstone

Claira Lloyd

Geoff Lloyd

Thea Loch

Kim Locke

Karen Lomas

Jacky Long

Danielle Lonnon

Dagan & Erin Lonsdale

Fem Loos

Ed & Deb Loucks

John New & Deborah

Lough
Victoria Clare Louise
Judith S. Loukides
Jennifer Lowerre
Kayla Lowes
David Luke
Julie Lush
Susan Lymn
Steph Lynch
Fabian Müller
Abby MacArthur
Kate Macnamara
J. E. & N. Madsen
Susan Maguire
Rhonda Maguire
Geraldine Mallon
Debra Mandel
Sara Mandel
Emily Manning
Michele Manns
Abi Marchant
Claudia Margach
Nicole Marino
Mark & Daya
Emily Marks
Sarah Marlin
Shuna Marr
Mark & Ramona
    Martin
Jackie Martin-Corben
Paul Maskens
Kathryn & Alex Mather
Francine Matthews
Michael Matthews
Sophie Mautner

Leigh Mawson
Nathaniel Mawson
Hayley May
Annie Mayes
Shaun McAlister
Sam McAuley
Gemma McCafferty
Marie McCafferty
Samm McCandless
Mary Ellen McCann
Madeleine McColgan
Ailsa McCullagh
Rod McDonald
Cat McDonald
Louisa McDonnell
Susan McDougall
David McFadzean
Lucy & Nick McGill
Malcolm McGrath
Kathryn McGrath
Sarah McIlwaine
Helen & Gerard
    McInerney
Carole McIntosh
Andrew McIver
Michael Brian
    McKenna
Gavin McKeown
Palma McKeown
Louise McLaren
Bob McLaughlin
Sharne McLean
Megan McLeod
Karen Mcmahon
Kevin McNally

Becca & Greg
    McQueen
Gavin Meek
Susana Maria Menezes
Mr and Mrs Merel
Michel Meyers
Krister M. Michl
Louise Mijatovic
Bette Miles-Holleman
Alan Millar
Avery Miller
Beverly J. Miller
Derek Miller
Karen Millward
Karl Minns
Rakesh Mistry
Sue Mitchell
Karen Mitchell
Trish Mitchell
Martel Mitchell
Ruth Mitchell &
    Shai Walters
Charles & Lauren
    Modica
J. Moe
Hazel Monger
Tom Moody-Stuart
Anna Moogk
Jim Mooney
Dave Moore
Alison Mordue
Caitlyn & Peter
    Morgan
Clare Morgan
    (almost Digby)

Andrea Morley
Chris Morley
Dorothy Morton
Jane Morton
Naomi Mott
Simon Moulden
Alex Mozes
Kieran Mulchrone
Karen Muldoon
Rik Muller
Patrick Mullin
Caz Mumin
Duncan & Becca
    Munday
Angus & Deborah
    Munday
Duncan & Becca
    Munday
Angus & Deborah
    Munday
Sean Murphy
Sarah Murray
James Stacey Murray
Deborah Myrick
Lydia Ndoinjeh
Andrew Neve
Paula Newens
Paula Newens
Andy Nichol
Al Nicholson
Christopher Nielsen
Babs Nienhuis
Candice Nightingale
Malin Nilsson
Frances Niven

Anita North
Stewart & Arlene
    Norton
Herat
    Numberthirtyeight
Vicky Nunn
Esther Nwanuforo
Fiona O'Driscoll
Helen O'Keeffe
Celia O'Meara
Susan O'Neill
Cathelijne Olderaan
Eloise Oldershaw
Giselle Borg Olivier
Linda Olsson
Kaylene ONeill
Jane Ormerod-
    Wilkinson
David Orrison
Julia Osborn
David & Dianne
    Osborne
Pip Ostell
David Overend
Cheryl Owen
Tannia Owens
Harry Oxley
Patricia Paddock
Jan Page
Martin Paige
Karen Painter
Camelia Pall
Tracey Pallett
Alison Rayner Palmer
Laura Parascani

Allison Parish
Sue Park
Julia Parker
Kevin Parker
Mike Parkinson-Brown
David Parry
Amanda Paterson
Jade Paton
Ellie Patterson
Irene Paul
Rory Paxton
Jonathan & Jennifer
    Paxton
Carrie Peacock
Rachel Peck
Steph & Paul Pederson
Claire Peebles
Gemma Perry
Sarah Perry
Gemma Peters
Alex Petrie
Caroline Philpott
James Phyland
William Pickwell
Nathalie Pineau
Matthieu Pinel
Fay Poate
Liz Pollard
Justin Pollard
Nell Pols
Casey Poon
Tammy Poon
Rebecca Pope
Johan Pordon
Vie Portland

Sarah Potten
Gudrun Pötzelberger
Andie Powell
Mackenzie Powers
Montse Pratsobrerroca
Deborah Preston
Samina Price
Christopher Pridham
Arthur Prior
Jenny Pryer
Samuel Pryor
PubUtopia.com
   (UK pub guide)
John Pullan
Paivi Punnonen
Joanna Purdue
Pradesha
   Puvanendiranathan
Mikael Qvarfordh
Joachim Røberg-Larsen
Paul Raymond
Colette Reap
Madison Reid
Helen Reid
Laura Reilly
Beverley Revill
Kate Richards
Kathryn Richards
Mark Richards
Alison Riches
Kirsty Rickett
Adriana & Jonny
   Roberts
Debby Roberts
Jane Roberts

Julie Roberts
Bev Roberts
Hazel Robertson
Ian Robertson
Amanda Robinson
Jane Robinson
Benn Robinson
Samantha Robinson
Frank Rodolf
Liz & Mike Rodwell
Indigo May Roe
Felicitas Rohder
Amoreli Ronquillo
Andrew V. Rose
Ira Rosenblatt
Suzanne Rosewell
Catherine Rossi
Agnes Rotger
Ala Rothwell
Claire Royall
Gemma Russ
Allan P. Russell
Samantha Russell
Debbie Russell
Marie Ryal
Kevin & Kate Ryan
Emma Rycroft
Paul Sadler
Jonathan Sala
Laura Sale
Lynn Salls
Stephen Salter
Gur Samuel
Christoph Sander
Jill Sanders

Nik Sargent
Karen Sargent
Timothy Sawyer
Neil Scales
Tamara Schermer
Jessica Schneider
Miranda Schuchhard
Paul Scovell
Catherine Scully
Anne Seabright
Michael Seaton
Katherine Setchell
Mathew Sforcina
Moira Shaw
Andy Sheard
Miriam Sheppard
Helen Sherman
Lindy Sherwell
James Sherwood
Laura Shively
Louise Shortt
Gareth & Sylvia
   Silvanus
Maurilo Silveira
Sue Simmons
Marie Simpson
Neil Simpson
Aleksandra Siuda
Rhona & Sharon Skene
Emma Skinner
Stephen Slade
Lesley Sloss
Rieke Smakman
Rachel Smart
Martin Smedley

Amy Smiles
Dawn & Damian Smith
Sarah & Mark Smith
Jonathan Smith
Nathan Smith
Alyson J. J. Smith
Carol Smyth
Lee Snook
Lili Soh
Anne Soilleux
Fiona Sothcott
Oksana John Souter
Barbara Southby
Hilary Spence
Leo Spesshardt
Lorna Spracklin
Brett St.Clair
Debi Staron
Sofie Stenvall
Ros Stern
Annie Stevens
Nikki Stevens
Jessica Stevenson
Stuart Stickland
Lauren Stimpson
Lynnzie Stirling
Ian Stokoe
Adam Stone
Deborah Striegel
Heather Derouso
Davin Strong
Deborah Stubbs
Michael Styan
Edmund Sumbar
Emma Summers

Andrew Sunnucks
Noora Svensk
Samuel Sweetman
Marietta Szczalba
Ken Tague
Trina Talma
Helen Taylor
Alan Teixeira
Martin & Deborah
    Terry
Plinks Thomas
Barbara Thomas
Carole Thomas
Sian Thomas
Allison Thompson
Julie Thompson
Sharon Thomson
Sarah Thorpe
François Thunus
Caroline Tillotson
Linda Todd
Bryan Toesland
Alex Toufexis
Sheryl Townsend
Pete Trace
Bethanie Tranter
Trav Travster
Stephen Trepanier
Alex Trickett
Phil Trouteaud
Laura Tryphonopoulos
David Tubby
Paul & Catherine Tuli
The Great Twazu
Anne Tweed

Sarah Uldricks
Anthony Usher
Nathalie van Camp
Paul van der Star
Martijn van Es
Joy van Lieshout
Karin van Lon-Nissink
Laurens van Piggelen
Geert Vangenechten
Christine Varey-Brown
Tony 'The Big Dog'
    Varughese
Peter Vaughan
Kearan Vayro-Lennard
Deyanira Verdejo
Anastasia Vesperman
Sue Vincent
Ian Voller
Andrew Waddington
Mike Wade
Linda Verstraten &
    Pyter Wagenaar
Jennifer Wagner
Donalda Wain
Christopher Walker
Nigel Walker
Samuel Walker
Edward Walker
Jason Walker
Alister Walsh
Karin Wannemacher
Katherine Ward
Nickie Ward
Yasuko Watanabe
Simon Watchorn

Nichola Waterhouse

Christine Watkinson

Sue Watson

Nicola Watson

Andrea Watson

Sue Watson

Angela Watt

Tanya Weaver

Steve Webb

Julie Webster

Warren Weertman

Ian Weir

Lorna Weller

Hannah West

Erin Whiley

Lena Whitaker

Helen White

Karen Whitehead

Elinor Whitehouse

Christine Whitmore

Sue Whitney

Jon Wicks

Mattias Widmarl

Madeleine Wilkie

Karen Wilkins

!ewis Wilkinson

Susan Williams

Melissa Williams

Alan Williams

Rebecca Williams

Claudia @cyopro
    Williams

Kathy Williams

Michelle Williamson

Michelle Willis

Sarah Willoughby

Deborah Wise

Steffi Wode

Ingrid Wong

Debbie Wood

Aaron Wood

Karen Wood

Elizabeth Wood

Carol Woodward

Steve Woodward

Jill Woolf

Gillian Worrall

Simon & Lorna Wright

Daniel Wright

Alexander Wright

Diny Wright

Alan Wright

Barbara Wyant

Anita Wyss

Kumba Yamba

Emmy Yeadon

Riana Yeates

Andrew Yew

Simon York

Craig Young

Brecht Yperman

Sergey & Anna Yurkov

Jane Zara

Gregory Zayia

@Quipidity

@Katspjamas

@adverseken

@Riddlebrick

@HmtheJames

@49gimel

@WeeManUpNorth

@Mrs2Belly

And with special thanks to our friends at
www.debts-homes-kids.co.uk
for all their support.

A Note About The Typefaces

THE body text of the book is set in Perpetua 11 / 13½ pt. The typeface was designed in 1925 by Eric Gill (1882–1940), an eccentric sculptor, printmaker and designer whose roots were in the Arts and Craft movement. Perpetua has a chiselled, neo-classical quality that derives from Gill's fondness for stone engraving.

The page and section titling is set in Gill Sans, another Gill typeface that was in part inspired by the Johnston typeface used across the London Underground which Gill worked on as an apprentice.

The recipes are set in his 1931 typeface Joanna, described by Gill as 'a book face free from all fancy business'.